A PLAN of NEWCASTLE

THE INGENIOUS BEILBYS

1, 2 The Fitzwilliam Royal Goblet
Front (left)
Bucket bowl with opaque spiral twist stem. Normal foot.
Height $8\frac{1}{4}$ in.
Decor: The Royal Arms of George III in full colour enamel with gilt rim.
The Fitzwilliam Museum, Cambridge.

Reverse (right)
Decor: The Prince of Wales Arms in full colour enamel, with the signature
WBeilby Junr NCastle inv^t & pinx^t.
1762 (assumed date)
Photograph
Photo-Mayo

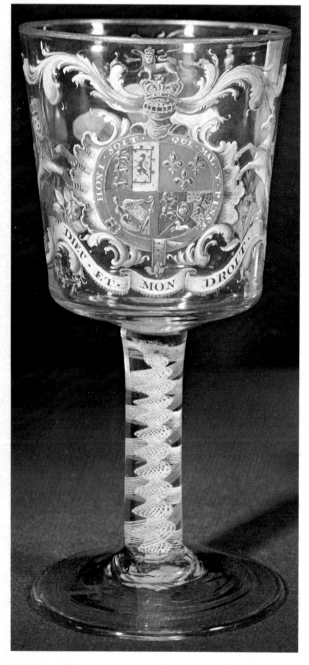

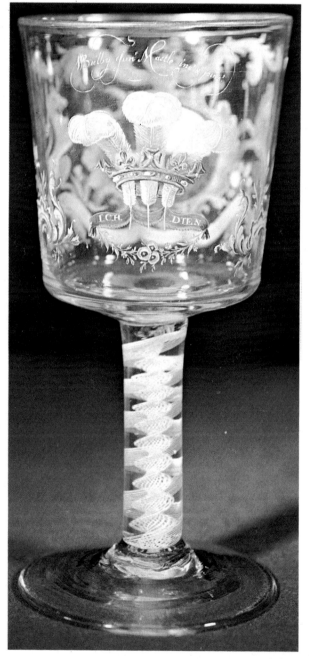

2

THE INGENIOUS BEILBYS

James Rush AFC, FRSA

BARRIE & JENKINS LONDON

© 1973 by James Rush

First published 1973 in Great Britain by
Barrie & Jenkins Ltd
24 Highbury Crescent, London N5 1RX

ISBN 0 214 65412 5
Designed and printed in Great Britain
at The Curwen Press, Plaistow, London E13 9HJ

Contents

5

List of Illustrations

All glassware reproduced in this book is authentic
Newcastle Glass of the eighteenth century, and, with
the exception of the glassware reproduced in plate 96,
can be attributed to the Beilbys. The caption states
if the glass is signed, or dated.

8

Newcastle Courant, 4 July 1778

'Died Sunday, Mrs Beilby, mother of
the ingenious Beilbys of this town.'

3 The Pembroke Goblets
Each of similar decor but
illustrated showing front
and reverse.
(a) Bucket bowl with opaque
twist stem and normal foot.
Height $8\frac{5}{8}$ in.
Decor (front) The Arms of
the Earl of Pembroke and
Montgomery in red, azure
and gold. Gilt rim.

(b) Bucket bowl, with opaque
twist stem and normal foot.
Height $8\frac{1}{2}$ in.
Decor (reverse): The
Pembroke Crest, a Wyvern
Vert with supporting
rococo scroll in colour
enamels.
Decorated by William
Beilby and signed on
reverse *Beilby Invt & Pinxt*.

Circa 1765
The Corning Museum of
Glass, New York
Photograph
Stanley Weisenfeld

10

Preface

The 'ingenious Beilbys' – a modest tribute in a modest circumspect decade. But perhaps 'fabulous' would have been a better word in the light of reluctant history. Who were the Beilbys, and how did they become 'ingenious' and perhaps 'fabulous'?

To the people of England, and particularly to those from the North of England, the name means nothing. Ask any average person in the streets of London and Newcastle upon Tyne, and ninety-nine times out of a hundred, the answer would be: 'Never heard of them'. Yet this family, William, Ralph and Mary Beilby, were destined to become truly fabulous and famous to art connoisseurs throughout the world, a fame of which, in their simple way of life during the late eighteenth century, they were unaware.

As an important addition to the three Beilbys comes a fourth figure, who can be considered almost an honorary member of the family, and who has, in fact, achieved world fame: Thomas Bewick, the great wood-engraver, who at the age of fourteen, became apprenticed to Ralph Beilby. The fame of Thomas Bewick has to some extent over-shadowed the work of the Beilby family, but nevertheless the association is important; and from this association have come the most charming and revealing anecdotes of the period.

This, then, is the story of the Beilbys. The decorators of glassware, the artists, the technicians in glass perfection – so much so that their work is exhibited in all the great museums of the world. A single authentic Royal piece of glass decorated by William Beilby would today fetch at Sotheby's in London anything from six to ten thousand pounds.

The Beilbys' story is a fascinating one; it is a great saga. It is also one of mystery and conjecture. Most of what I have learned about the Beilbys comes from intensive research in museums, libraries, countless parish records and the study of old glass houses, maps and voluminous correspondence, almost without end. I have followed many blank trails and come up against almost unbelievable obstruction at times, but still the story comes through, its message clear and firm.

It is not only a story of a family, it is also the story of a city, the

11

city of Newcastle upon Tyne. Today most people talk about New-castle as a black industrial city and think of it only in terms of coal. With respect, Southerners are contemptuous and speak of Newcastle in tones of pity for one living and working there. And yet, from this 'Black Prince of a City', as H. V. Morton once called it, have come these remarkable and almost priceless works of art, known as 'Beilby' glass. Not only that; from Newcastle upon Tyne has come the glory of a great age in glass, the glory of the eighteenth century, the great Light Baluster period of Newcastle Glass.

And so, this book is most humbly written and dedicated to the memory of the Beilbys and also to the memory and glory of a great period for the city of Newcastle upon Tyne.

I very much regret that after so much research, many questions remain unanswered, but I trust that after the publication of this book, much thought will be stimulated, and from the people of the North will come some of the answers.

But, whatever the failings of the written story, I feel that it must be transcended and ultimately fulfilled by the great beauty of the photography which conveys, as no written word possibly can, the true glory of 'The Ingenious Beilbys'.

JAMES RUSH
Newcastle 1972

Acknowledgements

The author desires to place on record his sincere appreciation of the following persons and organizations, without whose co-operation and help the writing of this book would have been quite impossible.

MR B. COLLINGWOOD STEPHENSON, MA, FMA, FRSA, Director of The Laing Art Gallery, Newcastle upon Tyne, for his kind encouragement and permission to photograph the Beilby specimens.

MISS M. A. V. GILL, of the Glass and Ceramics Section of The Laing Art Gallery, for her assistance in correction and identification.

MR F. R. WOODWARD, BSC, FSA(Scot), Curator of The Shipley Art Gallery, Gateshead, for permission to photograph and reproduce the glass processional novelties illustrated in 'The Happy Glassmakers' chapter.

THE REVEREND R. H. GURNEY, Rector of St Mary's Church, Gateshead, for permission to photograph the Timothy Tyzack Memorial Tombstone.

MISS SUSAN BOOTH, of The Ashmolean Museum, Oxford, for arranging the photography of the 'Tho. Brown' Flask and for permission to reproduce it.

MR HUGH TAIT, FSA, Keeper of the Department of Medieval and Later Antiquities, British Museum, for his kind help in research.

MR W. A. TAYLOR, MC, FLA, City Librarian, Birmingham Reference Library, for help in research.

MR L. M. BICKERTON, FLA, FMA, Curator of the Worthing Museum and Art Gallery, for his encouragement and help in research.

THE DIRECTORS OF THE WILKINSON SWORD COMPANY LIMITED for their permission to photograph and reproduce the Beilby glass 'Success to the Swordmakers'.

THE EARL OF WESTMORLAND, KCVO and MR A. J. B. KIDDELL, of Sotheby's in London, for their encouragement and practical help.

MRS HANS LESSER, who read the manuscript and gave important advice and encouragement.

MR ROBIN M. GARD, MA, County Archivist of Northumberland, and his staff, for their unstinting co-operation in research.

14

THE STAFF OF NEWCASTLE CENTRAL LIBRARY REFERENCE SECTION for their very cheerful and willing co-operation in research over a considerable period of time.

MISS J. W. THOMPSON, FLA, of Newcastle Central Library, for her immense help in research and for her reading and advice in preparing the manuscript.

MRS R. COULSON SCORRER of Newcastle upon Tyne, for her kind permission to reproduce her late husband's excellent drawings of old Newcastle.

MR DAVID BOURNE, Secretary of the Newcastle upon Tyne Society of Antiquaries, for placing at my disposal the archives of the Society and for permission to use the excellent reference library at the Black Gate Museum, Newcastle.

MR J. K. BISHOP, City Archivist, City and County of Newcastle upon Tyne, for placing at my disposal the City Archives.

DR J. M. FEWSTER, University of Durham, Department of Palaeography, for his kind co-operation in research.

MR CHARLES P. NEAT, Member of the Society of Genealogists, Durham, for his laborious searches in Durham on my behalf.

MR DEREK C. DAVIS, Glass Connoisseur of London, for his immense help and advice in research and locating of Beilby pieces, and also for reading and appraisal of the final manuscript.

MISS SHEILA PITCAIRN, Genealogist, of Dunfermline, Fife, Scotland, for her painstaking searches of archives and parish records in Fifeshire and Scotland.

MR J. P. PALMER, Keeper of Applied Arts, The Fitzwilliam Museum, Cambridge, and to his staff for the splendid help in photographing their Beilby specimens and for permission to reproduce them.

MAJOR F. J. CHARLTON and MRS CHARLTON of Hesleyside, Northumberland, for their kind hospitality and co-operation with the chapter 'The Standard of Hesleyside'.

MR L. H. HARWOOD, ARICS, QALAS, of The National Trust, for his kind permission to photograph and reproduce the painting *The Spur in the Dish* at Wallington Hall.

MR D. J. BRYANT, FLA, of The Kingston upon Hull Central Library for his co-operation in research.

DR JOYCE M. BELLAMY of the University of Hull, for her assistance in research at Hull.

MISS MARGARET GREENSHIELDS of The Cecil Higgins Art Gallery, for her splendid help in photographing the Beilby specimens under her charge, and for permission to reproduce them.

MR CHARLES PARISH, FLA, of The Literary and Philosophical Society, Newcastle upon Tyne, for making available certain of the archives of the Society for study and for permission to reproduce the 'Mrs Ralph Beilby Letter'.

The following private collectors of glass for their hospitality, enthusiasm and great willingness to help photograph their specimens:

THE HON. MRS R. J. P. WYATT

MR R. S. LYMBERY

MR K. A. ALEXANDER

MR PAUL N. PERROT, Director of The Corning Museum of Glass, New York, for arranging the photography and granting permission to reproduce certain of the Beilby glass specimens in his charge.

MR CALVIN S. HATHAWAY, Curator of Decorative Arts, Philadelphia Museum of Art, for arranging the photography and for granting permission to reproduce the Beilby specimens.

MISS RUTH HURST VOSE of The Pilkington Glass Museum, St Helen's, Lancashire, for her help in photographing the Beilby pieces in the Museum and for arranging permission to reproduce them.

MR R. J. CHARLESTON, Keeper, Department of Ceramics, The Victoria and Albert Museum, for his kind permission to photograph and reproduce the many Beilby specimens in the museum.

DR NEVILLE WILLIAMS, of the Public Records Office, London, for his help in obtaining the reproduction of Ralph Beilby's signature.

MR R. BRIAN BAIRD, for his professional advice and public relations service.

THE RIGHT WORSHIPFUL LORD MAYOR OF NEWCASTLE UPON TYNE, ALDERMAN ARTHUR GREY, CBE, for his personal encouragement, and for his good offices in arranging the Reception for the subscribers to the Limited Edition.

16

Part One 1 Newcastle glory

Newcastle upon Tyne and its immediate area, in the eighteenth century, was to become one of the largest and most famous glass-producing centres of the world. In the great hey-day of Newcastle Glass, no fewer than thirty-two glass houses were situated and fully employed in the area.

Just emerging from the Middle Ages, Newcastle was an attractive walled medieval city, planned as a fortress around the Norman castle, built by the son of William the Conqueror and from which it was to receive its famous name, the 'NEW CASTLE' (see plate 5).

It is perhaps fitting that the great era of Newcastle Glass should commence with a Royal edict. This was the Royal Proclamation in the thirteenth year of the reign of King James in 1615, in which was 'prohibited the making of glafs with wood firing for the better preferving of timber'. Thus it was that the lovely forests of late medieval England were saved from the ravages of the glassmakers, who had depended almost entirely on the availability of wood as fuel for their all-consuming furnaces.

The new challenge of making glass was taken up by a totally un-expected champion – a King's favourite – Admiral Sir Robert Mansell who was, in fact, 'the man of the hour', and who was to succeed beyond his wildest dreams.

It is strange indeed that King James had misgivings about the suitability of Sir Robert's appointment, for on 5 March 1619 he was heard to observe that he 'wondered Robert Mansell, being a feaman, whereby he had got fo much honour, fhould fall from water to tamper with fire, which are two contrary clements'.

Sir Robert turned instinctively towards the only true alternative fuel supply – coal. His first efforts were technically unsuccessful. Welsh, Scottish and Nottingham coal was tried, but all failed be-cause of the high cost of transportation and the effects of sulphur in the glass melt. Then suddenly came *Newcastle* and success. 'For his last refuge, he was enforced to make triall at Newcastle upon Tyne, where, after the expenditure of many thousand pounds, that work for glafs was affected with Newcastle cole.'

The fine geographic location of Newcastle upon Tyne was the

17

ultimate deciding factor. It was the largest coal producing centre in the world, and because of the River Tyne it had easy access to the Thames and to the markets of the world.

5 The medieval fortress of Newcastle upon Tyne The south-west corner of the medieval fortress of Newcastle upon Tyne as it would have appeared in the reign of King James in 1615.

The Whitefriars Tower is in the foreground, whilst in the background, to the right, is the 'New' Castle. *Etching by* R. Coulson Scorrer

18

6 Decanter
Sloping shoulder decanter
in flint glass with cut
stopper.
Height $10\frac{7}{16}$ in. (including
stopper)
Decor: Unidentified Arms
in colour enamel, supported
by scroll and fruiting vine
in white enamel. Beilby
butterfly on neck.

Decorated by William
Beilby.
Circa 1770
The Corning Museum of
Glass, New York
Photograph
Stanley Weisenfeld

7 Goblet
Bucket bowl with opaque
twist stem. Normal foot.
Height 7 in.
Decor: Pyramid and
classical ruins in white
enamel. Gilt rim.
Circa 1770
Mr R. S. Lymbery
Photograph
Photo-Mayo

19

2 The Huguenots
'Gentilhommes Verriers' *

Gentlemen Glassmakers of Lorraine

The first essay of glassmaking on the banks of the Tyne was not initially achieved by Sir Robert Mansell. During the sixteenth century, there had developed in Lorraine, Northern France, quite a considerable glass industry. The glassmakers of Lorraine were almost entirely Protestant and came from the three great noble families of De Hennezel, De Thietry and Du Thisac, the gentlemen glassmakers of Lorraine. These three names were afterwards anglicized to Hensay, Tyttery and Tyzack. As a result of their religious persecution, culminating in the infamous St Bartholomew massacre of 1572, many of these glassmakers emigrated to England to establish themselves in a new way of life and to continue their craft as glassmakers.

The first of the Huguenots arrived in the Newcastle upon Tyne area during the reign of Queen Elizabeth I, and they endeavoured to establish themselves as glassmakers in the area of Newcastle upon Tyne called 'The Close', very near to the old City Wall and the towering edifice of Closegate, which barred the entrance to Newcastle upon Tyne along the Close (see plates 16, 17 and 18). The attraction of this site was the off-loading availability of coal – their only source of fuel – from the nearby Skinnerburn, or Skinnerbourne.

This venture of the hapless Huguenots did not meet with the success it deserved, and for one reason or another, they abandoned what was, in fact, a perfect site which afterwards was to be re-established as one of the great centres of glassmaking by the Dagnia family.

The Huguenots apparently wandered throughout England for some time, and even worked as glassmakers in the Stourbridge area, but then came the advent of Sir Robert Mansell and the ultimate granting to him of a Royal Monopoly for the manufacture of glass in England in 1623.

Before he had been granted this monopoly, Sir Robert Mansell had already moved and established the first authenticated glassworks in Newcastle upon Tyne at the site of the Ouseburn in 1619. This site was as ideal in the east of Newcastle upon Tyne as the Closegate and Skinnerburn were in the west.

* Gentlemen Glassmakers

Thus for the next two hundred years we find that the glassware industry of Newcastle upon Tyne developed in two distinct sites; to the west, the Closegate area, which was to be developed by the great Dagnia family, and in the east, the Ouseburn area, the much larger site to be developed by the Huguenots under the guidance and authority of Sir Robert Mansell.

This Ouseburn site is still represented by name today. Glasshouse Street runs along the side of the Tyne, while on the tributary of the Ouse, just at the point where it reaches the River Tyne, is the Bridge across the Ouse which is called the Glasshouse Bridge.

Once again, access was the vital factor; the coal was carried in the shallow-bottomed keelboats for the glass houses and these were also used to despatch the finished glass by way of the Tyne to the Thames and to the world markets (see plate 8).

Sir Robert Mansell had selected well in his choice of site, but his organizing genius had recognized the importance of the 'gentlemen glassmakers of Lorraine', and the first of the great families were brought to the Ouseburn. Their names still survive in Newcastle upon Tyne and on Tyneside today. They were, quoting from the records of the time: 'Tymothy Teswicke, glaſsmaker, a Frenchman', 'Isaack Henzey, glaſsmaker' and 'his brother Jacob Henzey'. An

8 Keelboats on the Tyne
Reproduced from an original woodcut by Thomas Bewick, this picture gives a good impression of what the Tyne keelboats were like. The scene is set very close to where Thomas Bewick was born on the banks of the Tyne near Mickley.

21

9 Three wine glasses
Assumed by the author to
be the work of Mary Beilby.
Circa 1770
(a) Round funnel with rare
blue cord and opaque twist
stem.
Height $6\frac{3}{4}$ in.
Decor: Fruiting vine in
white enamel. Gilt rim.

(b) Drawn stem ratafia
glass with trumpet bowl.
Height $7\frac{1}{4}$ in.
Decor: Scroll in white
enamel. The lower portion
of the bowl has a very rare
decoration of diminishing
blue pearls. Gilt rim.

(c) Ogee bowl wine glass
with opaque twist stem.
Height $5\frac{7}{16}$ in.
Decor: Simple scroll in
white enamel.
The Corning Museum of
Glass, New York
Photograph
Stanley Weisenfeld

22

10 The Horsey wine glasses
Ogee bowl with opaque twist stem and normal foot.
(a) Height $7\frac{1}{4}$ in.
(b) Height $5\frac{1}{4}$ in.
Decor: The Cypher and Crest of the Horsey family in yellow and brown enamel. The Cypher initials are L.M.H. and the Crest is a representation of a horse's head. Both glasses have worn gilt rims. Decoration assumed to be by William Beilby.
Circa 1775
The Corning Museum of Glass, New York
Photograph
Stanley Weisenfeld

23

interesting addition was the name 'David Tyttere, alias Rusher, glafsmaker' (this last name was later to be anglicized to Rush). Thus the three noble glassmaker families of Lorraine were established at Ouseburn and it is important perhaps to note the difference in spelling gradually brought about by English influence; Henzey became Henzell, Tyzack remained Tyzack and Tyttere became Titterie, then Tyttery. Why David Tyttere assumed his alias of *Rusher* is something of a mystery but it may be that it was because he was afraid of the long arm of Lorraine vengeance, as many Protestants were under sentence of death during these difficult times, even if they had left the country.

An interesting discovery during the research of this period was to uncover the burial place of David Tyttere at All Saints' Church, only about half a mile from the Ouseburn. The record in the parish register reads: '1621 David Tyttery alias Rusher Gentleman and Glafsmaker.'

In the Ouse Valley there developed a flourishing industry under the control of Sir Robert Mansell, and in 1624 he had achieved an output of no less than four thousand cases of glass with three main furnaces working and sixty immigrant workmen. In 1640, during the occupation of the city of Newcastle upon Tyne by the Scots, Sir Robert informed Sir Francis Windebank, Secretary of State, that he had twelve hundred cases of glass there ready to be shipped to London.

The district had developed so intensively that during the eighteenth and nineteenth centuries the area was known as the Glasshouses. From the records of the historian Bourne, we find that in 1736 seven main glass houses had been established in this area: the Western Glass House, the Crown Glass House, the Middle Bottle House, the Middle Broad House, the Eastern Glass House, St Lawrence's or The Mushroom Glass House, St Lawrence's Bottle House.

The output from the glass houses was predominantly Crown glass, plate glass and bottle glass, but there is some evidence that certain fine quality items of flint glass were also produced. This fact has now been proved by the discovery of a magnificent crystal bowl made by John Henzell in 1756. It is engraved with the Henzell Arms and the name and date 'John Henzell 1756'. This could only have been made in one of the Ouseburn glass houses. This bowl was recently owned by a descendant of the family, Mr Charles W. Henzell of Tynemouth.

Throughout the Newcastle upon Tyne and Tyneside area one can today see gravestones and memorials to the presence of the Huguenots. One of the most interesting of these is the beautiful monumental stone alongside the High Altar of the Mother Church of Gateshead, St Mary's. The inscription reads:

'Here lyeth interred the body of Tymothy Tyzack,
Merchant Adventurer. 6th day of February, 1684.'

24

A photograph of this monument is shown in plate 11 and it will be observed that the coat of arms is that of the Henzell family, to whom the Tyzacks were related.

One of the early problems associated with the development of the Ouseburn glass houses was the difficulty in obtaining fire clay for the construction of the pots. Fortunately this was solved by the discovery of clay in Northumberland, near the village of Felton, and an indication of the growth of the Ouseburn glass houses can be gauged

11 Tombstone
The monumental tombstone of Tymothy Tyzack, glassmaker.
6 February, 1684.
Photographed to the left of the High Altar of St Mary's Church, Gateshead.
Photograph
Photo-Mayo

25

12

Although much later than the period of the early Huguenot glassmakers, John Brand's panorama, seen here, gives a wonderful impression of what the old town was like when Sir Robert Mansell decided on Newcastle as one of his great centres of glass production. On the extreme left can be seen the actual glass houses of the Dagnias at the Closegate with smoke belching forth. The Newcastle town wall can be clearly seen reaching down to the Closegate from the Whitefriars Tower. In the centre in the skyline is the Cathedral Church of St Nicholas, with the Castle just to the right, and the Tyne Bridge as repaired after the disastrous flood of 1771. The sailing vessels on the Tyne give a vivid picture of the period, but significant are the shallow keels which conveyed coal and glass to the markets of the world. In the foreground can be seen a loaded pit truck being lowered to the waiting keel-boats in the river. The pit pony, called locally a 'galloway' or 'cuddy', is being remotely controlled by the seated pitman on the truck. Far over to the right, just below the rising sun in the east, and only slightly off the picture, was the Glasshouse Bridge and the great conglomeration of glass houses by the Ousebourne which were founded by the Huguenots.

by the output of fire clay which was sold to the glassmakers: 1695 – 106 tons; 1762 – 188 tons; 1763 – 203 tons. It cost a mere £1 a ton.

The glassmakers of the Ouseburn were to follow the 'closed shop' tradition of their Huguenot ancestors. The author discovered the following revealing two documents in the archives of Northumberland County Council: 'Articles of agreement of supply of "blewy-glasse clay" to seven glassmakers of Newcastle, 1694, from the Thirston Bearfield pit (item 11); provided for 90 tons a year to be supplied by Edward Horsley Widdington for the next four years solely to Timothy Davison, Nicholas Fenwicke, Matthew White, Esquires, William Proctor, Jonathon Roddam, merchants, William Tizacke of the glass house "Broadmaker" and Joshua Middleton of

26

Drawn & Engrav'd by Ja.s Fittler

Sir Matthew White Ridley Bar.t Mayor,
County of the TOWN of NEWCASTLE upon TYNE, this View of that Town, taken
Engraved at their common Expence;
devoted faithful humble Servant, John Brand.

the glass house "Marcer", to be delivered at their glass houses called "The Westerhouses, Middlehouses, Easterhouses, Newhouse and Howdenpannes", and to none other save only "one tunne and noe more" to Daniel Titterie of the Haining Shoat Glass house, it being already "ordered him"'.

5th June, 1644. 'It is observed that the Henzells and Tyzacks ſtill continue to preſide over theſe glaſsworks – indeed they will admit none other of any other name to work with them.'

In concluding this chapter concerning the great part played by the Huguenots it is perhaps appropriate to quote the observation of the French writer Bernard Palissy: 'L'art de la Verrerie est noble et ceux qui y besognent sont noble.' ('Glassmaking is a noble art and those who practice it are noble.')

27

3 Admiral Sir Robert Mansell

Fourth son of Sir Edward Mansell of Margam. He became an Admiral of the Fleet and served with distinction at the siege of Cadiz in 1596 under the great Elizabethans Lord Howard of Effingham and the Earl of Essex. He was knighted in the same year by Queen Elizabeth and was a canopy bearer at the funeral of the great Queen at Westminster Abbey in 1619.

Sir Robert Mansell had done a magnificent job in establishing a glass industry in Newcastle; but everything did not go as smoothly as he would have liked.

He had struggled very hard to protect himself against infringements of his Royal Monopoly and was involved in many years of litigation. In most of this litigation he emerged successfully but it undoubtedly sapped his strength. His wife Lady Mansell was a tower of strength in these protracted legal wrangles and in his absence on Naval Duty fought hard and well in her husband's interests. In one brush with a counter-litigant she bitterly complained that she had lost £15,000 by her husband's integrity and loyalty.

Sir Robert ultimately won the battle in defence of his patents and rights as the following concluding paragraph of the Royal instrument shows:

'The premises considered, Sir Robert Mansell being out of purse so great a summe, with so great hazard, before hee could by any meanes or industry settle the busines to the benefit of the Commonwealth; and his Majesty taking the same into his Royall Consideration, as also the many and faithfull services of the sayd Sir Robert Mansell, by the advice of the whole body of his most Honorable Privy Councell, was graciously pleased to renew a Patent of priviledge to the sayd Sir Robert, as it before expressed: Wherefore he now resteth confident and humbly desireth that it will likewise stand with pleasure of his Honorable House, to ratifie what is done according to his Maiesties most Gracious intention, and thereby free him from that heavy imputation of contempt, undeservedly cast upon him by the sayd Petitioners. Vivat Rex.'

In 1635 King Charles I helped him materially by his Proclamation prohibiting the importation 'of any fort of glafs from foreign parts' during the monopoly granted him for the 'fole making of that commodity' by King James. In this proclamation King Charles lavishes praise.

'Sir Robert Mansell, had, by his industry and great expence, perfected that manufacture, with fea coal or pit coal, whereby not only the woods and timber of this Kingdon are greatly preferved, but the making of all kinds of glafs is eftablished here, to the faving of much treafure at home, and the employment of great numbers of our people.'

On 5 February 1637, the Corporation of Newcastle upon Tyne granted a new lease to Sir Robert:

'To Sir Robert Mansell, Knight, Vice Admiral of England. On confideration of the furrender of certaine grounds, being the greateft part of the eaft ballaft fhores and the glafshouses, and other feveral tenements erected upon the fame, and boundreth upon Ofeburne on the Weft. and extendeth itfelfe to a runnell betwixt the faid fhores and the grounds of St. Lawrence on the Eaft upon the river of Tyne, upon the fourth, unto a place called Statiford on the North part.' 5th of February 1637. 13 Charles I. 'Term of Michaelmas for 21 years at the yearly rent of 20 shillings' – not an exorbitant rent for such a vast tract of land along the banks of the Tyne.

But the twilight was fast falling on the declining days of the gallant Admiral. The great industry he had established began to suffer from civil unrest and with the advent of Cromwell and the Civil War of 1642, the wonderful period of prosperity had virtually ended. By the new order of things it was perhaps inevitable, when, in 1646, the monopoly granted to Sir Robert was ended.

On 17 July 1652, Sir Robert petitioned the Newcastle Common Council for a 'new leafe of the eaft ballast fhores and glafshoufes thereupon' but it is recorded 'his requeft was not complied with'.

On 12 August 1653, Admiral of England, Sir Robert Mansell died and soon afterwards it was recorded in the Newcastle upon Tyne Common Council Order Book that 'the remainder of his leafe, about six years, had devolved to one Mr. Moyer'.

And so, this was the end of a great beginning in Newcastle Glass.

In the archives of the City of Newcastle upon Tyne there is hardly any mention or true recognition of the great rôle Sir Robert Mansell played in its history, but the glass industry he had created on the banks of the Tyne and along the lovely, once green, valley of the Ouseburn was to continue through many vicissitudes to prosper again.

But perhaps the most important aspect of Sir Robert's work was the fact that he had established Newcastle upon Tyne as an industrial centre, with its great river access to the world markets. Not

29

13 Wine glass
Round funnel bowl, with opaque twist stem and normal foot.
Height 6 in.
Decor: Fruiting vine in white enamel with worn gilt rim.

Circa 1770
Bridge Glassworks, Newcastle upon Tyne
Photograph
Photo-Mayo

14 Wine glass
Ogee bowl with opaque twist stem and normal foot.
Height $6\frac{3}{8}$ in.
Decor: Peacock and Peahen in white enamel with pale blue acanthus scroll. Between the two birds are

two butterflies in flight. Thin gilt rim.
Circa 1770
The Pilkington Glass Museum, St Helen's
Photograph
Photo-Mayo

30

15 Decanter and ale glass
(a) *Decanter* Mallet type with ground stopper. Decor: The inscribed word *Beer* inside rococo scroll with hops and barley in white enamel. A typical Beilby butterfly on neck.

Height $10\frac{3}{4}$ in. (including stopper)
(b) *Ale glass* Elongated round funnel bowl and opaque twist stem and normal foot.
Height $7\frac{1}{4}$ in.
Decor: Hops and barley in white enamel.

Circa 1770
Fitzwilliam Museum, Cambridge
Photograph
Photo-Mayo

31

iron, but glass, says Baillie, was the richest branch of trade next to coal in Newcastle.

While Sir Robert worked alongside the Ouseburn, in the east, a new dynasty was being created in the west. To the natural site in the narrow confines of the Close, alongside another tributary access, to the Skinnerburn and the Closegate came the family of Dagnia. Indeed, to the very site abandoned by the Huguenot glassmakers. The Dagnia family, of Italian extraction, was to establish the true glory of Newcastle Glass and to herald the famous era of the Newcastle Light Baluster.

4 The Closegate

The Closegate was the area where the great glass houses of Newcastle upon Tyne were concentrated, particularly the two great flint glass houses of Williams and Company and Airey, Cookson and Company. The attractive etchings, by R. Coulson Scorrer, reproduced overleaf for the first time, graphically portray the area and recapture something of the atmosphere of medieval Newcastle.

Plate 16 illustrates the actual Closegate itself before it was demolished in 1797. It was roughly square, three storeys in height and was strongly fortified with great guns at the time of the Stuart Rebellion of 1745. In the etching, we are looking westward from inside the city wall. Beyond the Closegate to the west is the area known as 'Closegate Without' and the glass houses at the time of the Beilbys were situated each side of 'Closegate Without' as far west as the Skinnerburn.

The second etching, shown in plate 17, gives a magnificent impression of the Close after the Closegate was demolished in 1797. The thickness of the city wall on which the Closegate stood can clearly be seen. The Whitefriars Tower can be seen rising beyond the glass workers' house in the foreground. The picturesque Elizabethan houses 'within' the Close give a wonderful impression of the old Newcastle William Beilby loved, and where most of his greatest work was executed. The arched doorway on the right is the point where the Breakneck Stairs open out on to the Closegate, where William and Mary Beilby passed through on their favourite walk to the glass houses of Closegate.

The third etching, shown in plate 18, shows the Whitefriars Tower in its dominating position on the brink of the river bank. In the background can be seen the Castle. From the Whitefriars Tower can be seen the Breakneck Stairs, described in the chapter devoted to Mary Beilby.

33

The Close Gate (about 1790)
Designed from various sources

R Coulson Scorrer

17

after TMR   The White Friar Tower, from site of the Close Gate in 1826.   R Carlon Scorrer /33.

18

The assumed appearance of the White Friar Tower when in its complete state   R Carlon Scorrer.

35

5 The Glass Dynasty of Dagnia

The Dagnia Dynasty of Glass starts from about 1651 (see family tree in plate 20) when Edward Dagney, of immediate Italian descent, was born in Bristol and given the English Christian name of Edward. Very little is known of his early life, but he was described as 'Master Edward Dagney, an ingenious glassmaker' in 1651.

He was closely associated with an Englishman called John Williams, who was very much involved in the glass industry, and who was also a furnace maker. Technically, there were many difficulties in the Bristol area, particularly with the availability of fire clay for the glass furnace pots.

There is evidence that Edward Dagney carried out most of his early glassmaking in a wood-fired glass house in the Forest of Dean. A record exists of Edward going to this glass house with a certain Captain Buck in order to experiment with the smelting of iron in furnaces of 'glass house clay'. They were, however, unsuccessful. They had heard of the great advances being made in Newcastle upon Tyne and, in 1683, Edward Dagney left Bristol to re-establish his family fortunes on the Tyne. In 1684, together with his three sons Onesiphorus Dagney, Edward Dagney II and John Dagney, he had settled well in Newcastle and secured the 'lease of a messuage near Closegate for 999 years and erected thereon a glafshouse'. This was the very site, with more space in addition, to the area first tried by the Huguenots some years before.

Associated with the Dagneys in this enterprise were two other partners, Benejar Durant and J. Wall, but very little is known of them and they disappear from the records after 1691.

There is no record of the first Edward Dagney having died in Newcastle, and it is therefore probable that he died in Bristol before his sons were finally established in their new location.

Some time later the family name appears to have changed to Dagnia; but as late as 1726, according to the historian Bourne, the name was still Dagney. An interesting reproduction of an actual page from Bourne's *History of Newcastle* is shown in plate 19. It will be seen that the reference from 'Without the Closegate' goes on to state 'and a glafs-houfe to Mr. Dagney'.

36

19 A remarkable page extract from Bourne's *History of Newcastle*, published in 1726. Which is not only a vital reference to a 'glafshouse to Mr Dagney', but also a beautifully engraved record of the period.

CHAP. XII.

Of the Suburbs, and other out Places.

Sect. I.

Of the FORTH.

ITHOUT the *Close-Gate* is a pretty long Street, with Houses on each Side; which goes as far as a *Dike* called *Skinner-Bourne*, where are of late Years a Factory belonging to Mr. *Thomlinson*, a Pot-House to Mr. *Joseph Blenkinsop* and *Ralph Harl*, and a Glass-House to Mr. *Dagney*, and Company; from thence Northward at the Top of the Hill is the Place called the *Forth*, anciently called the *Frith*, which lies without the Walls of the Town, and abutts on the South on a certain little Close called *Goose-green-Close*, then it extends it-self to a Close called *Dove-cote-Close*, and from thence Westward by the fur-thest Ditch of the *Close*, which lies contiguous to the Corner of the Hedge, which is next to the Common Way which leads into the *Forth*. Then by and over the Common Way to the little Rivulet or Syke of Water in the Bottom of the Valley, and so passing the Syke, you go upwards to the Close called *Goose-green-Close*. The Forth contains 11 Acres of Ground. It was surveyed by Order of the Parliament, in the Year 1649, and valued at 12l. per Annum.

It was valued Tythe-free. The Town pay'd 4l. per Annum to the King for it.

How it comes to be called *Forth* or *Frith*, I can only conjecture. The Word ᶠ *Forth* or *Frith*, as it is anciently called, comes from the *Saxon* Word *Frith*, which signifies *Peace*. For the English *Saxons* held several Woods to be sacred, and made them *Sanctuaries*. From this Definition of the Word, it may be no improbable Conjecture that the ancient *Saxons* inhabiting about the Parts of the Wall where the Town now is, gave the Name of *Frith* to

ᶠ Blount Law Dictio-nary in verb. *Frith.*

P p   this

37

THE GLASS DYNASTY OF DAGNIA

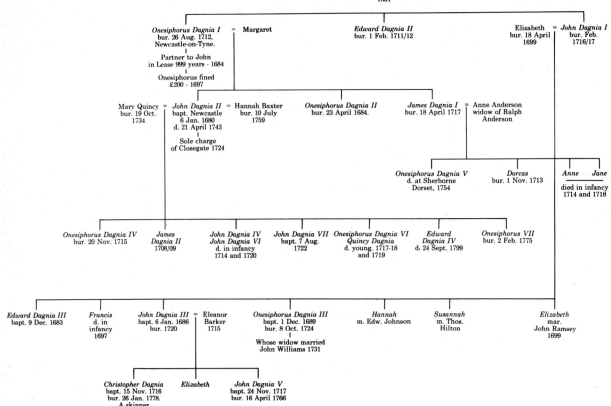

Edward Dagnia I, of Bristol, "Master Edward Dagney of Bristow, an ingenious glassmaker" 1651

Onesiphorus Dagnia I — Margaret, bur. 26 Aug. 1712, Newcastle-on-Tyne. Partner to John in Lease 999 years - 1684. Onesiphorus fined £200 - 1697

Edward Dagnia II, bur. 1 Feb. 1711/12

Elizabeth, bur. 18 April 1699 = John Dagnia I, bur. Feb. 1716/17

Mary Quincy, bur. 19 Oct. 1734 = John Dagnia II, bapt. Newcastle 6 Jan. 1680, d. 21 April 1743, Sole charge of Closegate 1724 = Hannah Baxter, bur. 10 July 1759

Onesiphorus Dagnia II, bur. 23 April 1684.

James Dagnia I, bur. 18 April 1717 = Anne Anderson, widow of Ralph Anderson

Onesiphorus Dagnia V, d. at Sherborne Dorset, 1754

Dorcas, bur. 1 Nov. 1713

Anne Jane — died in infancy 1714 and 1718

Onesiphorus Dagnia IV, bur. 20 Nov. 1715

James Dagnia II, 1708/09

John Dagnia IV / John Dagnia VI, d. in infancy 1714 and 1720

John Dagnia VII, bapt. 7 Aug. 1722

Onesiphorus Dagnia VI / Quincy Dagnia, d. young. 1717-18 and 1719

Edward Dagnia IV, d. 24 Sept. 1799

Onesiphorus VII, bur. 2 Feb. 1775

Edward Dagnia III, bapt. 9 Dec. 1683

Francis, d. in infancy 1697

John Dagnia III, bapt. 6 Jan. 1686, bur. 1720 = Eleanor Barker 1715

Onesiphorus Dagnia III, bapt. 1 Dec. 1689, bur. 8 Oct. 1724, Whose widow married John Williams 1731

Hannah, m. Edw. Johnson

Susannah, m. Thos. Hilton

Elizabeth, mar. John Ramsey 1699

Christopher Dagnia, bapt. 15 Nov. 1716, bur. 26 Jan. 1778. A skinner

Elizabeth

John Dagnia V, bapt. 24 Nov. 1717, bur. 16 April 1766

21 Wine glass and tumbler

(a) *Wine glass*
Ogee bowl with opaque spiral twist stem, and normal foot. Height 6¼ in.
Decor: Peacock and peahen in white enamel with rococo scroll in light blue. Worn gilt rim.
Circa 1765
(b) *Heavy bottom tumbler*
Height 4 in.
Decor: Exotic birds on tree in white enamel with Beilby butterfly on reverse side. Worn gilt rim.
Circa 1765
Fitzwilliam Museum, Cambridge
Photograph
Photo-Mayo

The most important aspect of the founding of the Dagnia glass house in the Closegate was the fact that this was, for the first time in Newcastle, specifically a flint glass house, and although the family was to extend its production to other fields of glass, such as window, Crown and bottle, it was this flint glassworks which was to make their name and fortune. Thus the Glass Dynasty of Dagnia was created and on this dynasty was founded the great Light Baluster Period of Newcastle Glass.

George Ravenscroft

In the meantime the Englishman George Ravenscroft had developed a revolutionary new process of making glass by the introduction of lead oxide into the melt. Under the tutelage of the Glass Sellers' Company of London he was ultimately to be granted a patent in 1676.

This process was to establish English glass as unassailable for brilliance and quality for many decades to come. The introduction of lead or flint was to give the glass a brilliant whiteness and it was also an ideal medium for cutting and decorating.

38

A Plan of NEW CASTLE upon Tyne and GATESHEAD 1788. Engraved by R. Beilby.

Front of the Publick Baths.

40

Engraving by Ralph Beilby. At Skinnerburn in the west the Dagnias were to reign supreme for over fifty years, while in the east at Ousebourne, the Huguenots, with the leading names of Henzell, Tyzack and Rusher, were to hold sway under Sir Robert Mansell.

To gain some impression of these sites, refer to the remarkable engraving of Newcastle upon Tyne by Ralph Beilby (plate 22) in 1788, after the destruction and rebuilding of the old Tyne Bridge in 1771. To the left, in the west, can be seen the Closegate (just by the printed word 'the') where the old city wall reaches down to the Close and the conglomeration of buildings each side of the Closegate Without to Skinnerburn, where the off-loading reach can clearly be seen.

Over to the east and right of the Beilby engraving can be seen the Ousebourne and the Glasshouse Bridge across it, near the Tyne, while alongside the river are clearly marked the 'High Glafs Houfes', the 'Middle Glafs Houfes' and, almost at St Anthony's the 'Low Glafs Houfes'. In the inset of Ralph Beilby's interesting engraving is another map of old 'New Castle' in 1610, when it was a medieval walled city and fortress.

41

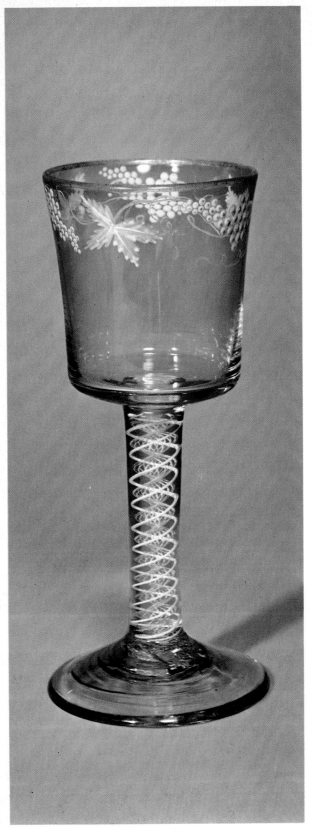

42

23 and 24 Two wine glasses
(a) Bucket bowl with opaque twist stem and folded foot.
Height $7\frac{11}{16}$ in.
Decor: Fruiting vine motif in white enamel. Gilt rim.
(b) Round funnel bowl with air twist stem and normal foot.
Height $6\frac{3}{8}$ in.
Decor: Garland scroll motif in white enamel with worn gilt rim.
Two glasses with interesting contrast. The bucket bowl glass with vine motif is undoubtedly by William Beilby whilst the round funnel is presumed to be the work of Mary Beilby.
Circa 1768
The Corning Museum of Glass, New York
Photograph
Stanley Weisenfeld

25 Decanter
Mallet-shaped decanter (without stopper) in flint glass.
Height $8\frac{7}{8}$ in.
Decor: Inscribed *W. WINE* with scroll and fruiting vine in white enamel. Beilby butterfly and scroll on neck in white enamel.
This decanter is one of a pair. The other being inscribed *PORT* and is in the same museum.
Decorated by William Beilby.
Circa 1770
The Corning Museum of Glass, New York
Photograph
Stanley Weisenfeld

43

The Dagnias in Newcastle upon Tyne were among the first to recognize the startling importance of this new advance in glassmaking and they were the first to establish a true flint glass works on the Tyne.

In 1681 the Ravenscroft monopoly ended and the Dagnias were to advance from strength to strength. The superb quality and craftsmanship of Newcastle Glass was now being recognized by London and by other world buyers. By 1701 four glass houses were established near the Closegate by the Dagnia family. There is no doubt that the great period of Newcastle Glass and the Light Baluster tradition started from this important year of 1701. The four Dagnia glass houses were all situated in the Closegate area, between the actual Gate across the Close and alongside an area called 'Closegate Without' to the Skinnerburn where the tiny tributary entered the Tyne; and where the main loading point for the Tyne keelboats was. At the Skinnerburn the raw materials, pot clay and silica sand, were off-loaded for the glass houses. The finished glass was loaded in the keels with coal as ballast to prevent undue movement of the glass packages.

By 1717 all the three Dagnia brothers were dead, but the important flint glass group was still maintained by the sons of John and Onesiphorus Dagnia. Ultimately, by 1724, John Dagnia II was in sole charge of the Closegate glass houses.

The year 1731 was an important date, one which was to mark the approaching twilight of the Dagnia Dynasty, for in that year John Dagnia introduced John Williams, the expert furnaceman, to the widow of his brother Onesiphorus III and after a somewhat peremptory courtship they married.

John Williams & Company
Later that year, John Williams was to assume full control of the Closegate flint glass house, while the Dagnias moved to South Shields, where their illustrious name was to be further enhanced by the creation of the first recorded 'paned' glass at Cleadon House. John Williams died in 1763, but the business continued as John Williams and Company. This flint glass house was to produce much fine glass but it was dogged by misfortune. One of the partners, Francis Rudston, became bankrupt in 1751, and this must have seriously retarded the development of the business. But worse was still to come.

In 1774, the main glass house was damaged by fire, but not seriously. The final disaster occurred in 1782, and the following graphic extract from the *Newcastle Courant*, dated 2 March 1782, tells the sad story:

44

'During a great part of Wednefday morning and that evening we had here violent gales of wind from the west quarter.

The same evening about fix o'clock, the wind blew down the roof of the Flint Glafs houfe, belonging to Meff. Williams and Co. in the Clofe at a time moft fortunate to the workmen who had a few minutes before defifting from their work and were thus providentially preferved from being buried in the ruins.'

Only two or three we are told were a little bruised.

'The roof falling upon the furnace foon caught fire and burnt with great violence until the whole building except a gable end was deftroyed. The violence of the wind created much fear for the fpreading of the flames to fome adjacent buildings which however was happily prevented by proper affiftance with a party of the militia now in quarters here.'

From this date, the records of John Williams and Company cease, and no trace can be found of any revival of their interests in the glass industry.

The Airey family

The Dagnia Dynasty in Newcastle was to last until 1728 when a well known and successful business man, Joseph Airey, was to acquire a lease and establish a new flint glass house in Closegate. Joseph Airey was a renowned Protestant dissenter and he built his glass house on the site of the Dissenters' Meeting House, almost alongside Closegate.

In Brand's *History of Newcastle* of 1789 there is this interesting entry: 'In the street that leads from Clofegate to Skinner-bourne, are several glafs houfes. One of thefe was formerly a meeting houfe of proteftant diffenters.'

In the research leading up to the publication of this book, considerable effort was made to find the actual location of this meeting house, and it was eventually found on a very tattered and worn map of old Newcastle by Corbridge in 1723. This map is not good enough for reproduction, but it quite definitely marks the site of the Protestant Meeting House with a cross just outside the Closegate.

There is also strong evidence to suggest that the Airey family of Newcastle were very much involved in the glass industry before the establishment of this glass house, for we have actually found a lease dated 1678:
' Leafe in Bitchfield of white clay and glafsmakers clay to Robert Roddam, John Airey and Peregrine Tizack. 19th April 1678.'

45

26 The Truth and Loyalty decanters (matched)
Sloping shoulder in flint glass. Rims ground for stoppers.
Height Left $9\frac{1}{4}$ in., Right $9\frac{15}{16}$ in.

Decor: Unidentified Arms in full colour enamel with scroll and fruiting vine in white. An inscribed motto *Truth and Loyalty* and the Beilby butterfly in white on the neck. These elegant decanters almost certainly

were produced in the glass-house of John Williams and Company and were decorated by William Beilby. The inscribing of the motto *Truth and Loyalty* is in the same writing and style of the authenticated signature

of William Beilby on the Royal Goblet in the Fitzwilliam Museum (plate 1).
Circa 1770
Philadelphia Museum of Art
Photograph
Alfred J. Wyatt

46

27 Wine glass
Trumpet bowl, drawn
opaque twist stem with
normal foot.
Height 7 in.
Decor: Fruiting vine in
white enamel. Traces of gilt
rim.

Circa 1770
Philadelphia Museum of Art
Photograph
Alfred J. Wyatt

47

6 The tax on glass and coal

The seventeenth-century war tax of 20 per cent on glass and coal was a devastating blow to the Newcastle glass industry and considerable hardship was felt among the workers and owners alike.

On 7 January 1696, a petition against the tax on glass and coal was presented to the House of Commons by Peregrine Henzell, John Henzell, Jacob Henzell and Peregrine Tizack, on behalf of themselves and the rest of the glassmakers on the North side of the River Tyne.

On 4 November 1698, Onesiphorus Dagnia, a glassmaker of Newcastle upon Tyne, was fined £200 and costs for having fraudulently concealed over 2,679 dozens of glass bottles.

When a further petition of the glassmakers of Newcastle was presented to the Crown on 21 May 1698, a much more moving picture is painted:

'Joshua Middleton, Owner of a Glass-house, said That he has endeavoured to strive with the burden of the said duty; and to that end kept his fire in and worked for twenty weeks, and employed his poor servants; but was forced to lay down, not being able to sell the glass he made, by reason of the addition the duty puts upon the price thereof; which puts so great a restraint upon their consumption; besides the loss they sustain in flying and breakage, after the duty is paid to the King. John Colt, Workman, said, He has left his wife and children behind him at Newcastle, whilst he came to seek for work in London; and has not had one day's work these 19 months, the fires being all out in the Country; but used to get 40s. a week when he was fully employed.'

The Glass Excise Act of 1745
The seventeenth-century tax on glass and coal had been partially repealed, but in 1745, the details of a new tax was to devastate the industry:
' For and upon all materials or metal of crown, plate and flint glaſs 9/4d for every hundredweight. For common bottle and green glaſs 2/4d for every hundredweight.'

And worse was yet to come, for by 1785 the tax on flint glass, which

48

of course included the finest quality crystal glass, was increased to $21/5\frac{1}{2}$d per hundredweight.

The glass industry was almost killed by this enactment. Apart from the increased price of coal, glassmakers were paying no less than 40 per cent of the price of the manufactured glass in duty. The scrimping of quality so that the manufacturers could sell at an economical price to pay this duty, made the base molten glass metal so foul and full of dross that it could barely be made into a saleable or acceptable article.

Perhaps the observation of W. A. Thorpe in 1929 was to summarize best the effect of this shattering excise act:
'Thus began the oppressive duties which hampered English glass-making for exactly a century, and ended by destroying the art of glass in England.'

49

7 The Newcastle Light Baluster

The glassmakers of Newcastle upon Tyne, to their eternal credit, did not take the blow of the Glass Excise Act lying down. So much so, in fact, that it was this Act that was to establish and to create the glory of the Newcastle Light Baluster era.

It was obvious that heavy tavern glass would be an uneconomical product after 1745, and the heavy baluster stems and the silesian stems, so popular on the continent, were definitely not economically viable. The Newcastle flint glass makers decided that superb quality and elegance was the only answer and so the Newcastle 'Light Baluster' was created.

A glance at the Newcastle Light Baluster in plate 28 clearly illustrates its striking and imposing style. The actual composition of the Newcastle 'metal' shows it to be homogeneous, crystal clear and without colour. Undoubtedly it discloses the Newcastle glassmakers to be masters of their craft and this specimen is enhanced by the subtle hand painting of William Beilby in a 'Fruiting Vine' motif.

Examining the baluster stem from which this famous style receives its name, one is impressed by the elegant balance it achieves, starting from the slender inverted baluster and combining with an angular knop close to the round funnel bowl. The inverted baluster shows a typical Newcastle characteristic in the lovely enclosed tears actually drawn into the stem.

There were many variations in the stem formations of Newcastle Light Balusters, but the fine example shown in plate 28 is a typical specimen.

Attention must also be drawn to the beautiful Newcastle Light Baluster decorated in colour enamel and signed by William Beilby. This outstanding example of the historic association between the Newcastle craftsmen in glass and William Beilby may be seen in the Victoria and Albert Museum, London. Colour photographs of it may be seen in plates 34 and 35.

One effect of the Glass Excise Act was to encourage the decorating of glass without weight and this in turn naturally developed the opaque and air twist stems, which also became an established feature of Newcastle Glass.

50

The final and greatest effect – so far as this book is concerned – was to establish the art of decorating glass by hand painting with colour enamels, and it was in this field that the Beilbys were to achieve fame.

The Newcastle Light Baluster period was to last from 1730, when the early baluster form was made, until, with the impetus of the excise tax, it was to achieve its largest demand in 1776, and production was gradually to come to an end in about 1785.

The Newcastle Light Baluster must be attributed to two flint glass houses of the period. The first was the flint glass house at Closegate, which was founded by the Dagnias and became Airey, Cookson & Company on the site of the old Protestant Dissenters' Meeting House. The second was the glass house, also founded by the Dagnias, in the Closegate approaching Skinnerburn which belonged to John Williams and Company, and which was destroyed by fire in the March of 1782.

Towards the end of the eighteenth century and early into the nineteenth century, good quality flint glass was produced in certain of the Ouseburn glass houses, particularly that of Richard Turner Shortridge and Company of North Shore. This firm still retained its link with the Huguenots through Joshua Henzell. In 1784, Joshua Henzell and James and Joseph King were declared bankrupt, but the business continued into the nineteenth century under the name of Richard Turner Shortridge. This financial disaster of Joshua Henzell must have been a very severe blow to the prestige of the famed glass family, and very little is subsequently heard of them in connection with the glass industry.

The development of the glass industry in Newcastle upon Tyne was to reach its peak by 1780, just about the time the work of the Beilbys came to an end. It was also virtually the end of the Newcastle Light Baluster era.

From the early tenuous efforts of the Huguenots to the greatness of Sir Robert Mansell – and through wonderful glass family names such as Dagnia, Cookson, Airey, Tyzack, Henzell and Rusher – the Newcastle glass industry had developed into one of the largest glass centres of the world.

In the great coal city of Newcastle upon Tyne itself, where the universal and graphic expression 'taking coals to Newcastle' had originated, the glass industry had become 'second only to coal' in size and importance.

51

28 Wine Glass
Newcastle Light Baluster
Round funnel bowl,
inverted light baluster stem
and normal foot.
Height $7\frac{1}{4}$ in.
Decor: Fruiting vine in
white enamel with thin gilt
rim.
Circa 1765
Fitzwilliam Museum,
Cambridge
Photograph
Photo-Mayo

29 Decanter
Sloping shoulder without
stopper.
Height $8\frac{7}{8}$ in.
Decor: The word
Mountain inscribed within
a scroll, in turquoise and
white enamel with a
supporting motif in fruiting
vine. A Beilby butterfly
appears in the neck.
Circa 1765
Victoria & Albert Museum,
London
Photograph
Photo-Mayo

52

8 The era of elegance in Newcastle glass

The Cooksons

When Joseph Airey built his glass house on the site of the old Dissenters' Meeting House at Closegate in 1728, the power of the Dagnias was virtually at an end, and this was to herald the advent of another famous glass family – the Cooksons.

The Cooksons had come to Newcastle upon Tyne in the seventeenth century from the Penrith area, and developed immense influence and power in the lead, iron founding and glass industries. John Dagnia, the son of Onesiphorus Dagnia, had acquired glass house properties at Cleadon in South Shields and this was to be sold to Isaac Cookson, thus establishing the Cookson Glassworks near the Mill Dam in South Shields. But the Cooksons' main development was the flint glass house at Closegate with Joseph Airey.

Isaac Cookson, the great financier of the Cookson family, was undoubtedly behind this development and his son John was actually apprenticed to Joseph Airey when the glass house was founded in 1728.

An indication of the power of the Cooksons is revealed in the London obituary notice of the death of Isaac Cookson: 'One of the most considerable glafs manufacturers in Newcastle'. He had already achieved eminence as Sheriff of Newcastle upon Tyne and he will be remembered in London as the most important virtual founder of Greenwich Hospital.

Airey, Cookson and Company

When the Meeting House was converted into a flint glass house, the firm was called Airey, Cookson & Co., for the rest of the eighteenth century.

The most significant discovery in recent researches by the author was to find the actual plans of the Airey, Cookson Glass House as established and working in 1802. This plan shows the exact location of the glass house and a reproduction of the plan is illustrated in plate 30. Referring to the right-hand side of the plan it can clearly be seen that the glass house was built right up to and alongside the old 'Town' Wall of the Walled City.

54

Until 1728 the Dagnia family had the virtual monopoly of flint glass production in Newcastle, and after the establishment of the Airey, Cookson & Company Glass House in Closegate, it was shared between the family representative, John Williams, and the rapidly developing power of Airey, Cookson and Company.

Most of the greatness and elegance of Newcastle Glass, and particularly the historic development of the Newcastle Light Baluster period, must be attributed to this vital period up to 1801. Credit for this must go in the name of the two flint glass houses already described, firstly what is clearly identified as Airey, Cookson & Company (with its now revealed exact location) and secondly, John Williams' Glass House, which must, almost certainly, have been in the area 'Without Closegate' – that is to say between Closegate itself and Skinnerburn, situated in the same area as about three other bottle and Crown glass houses. The location of this flint glass house belonging to John Williams cannot be precisely established.

Possible Excavation
There is no doubt that this area of the City of Newcastle is still rich for further research. At present it is heavily industrialized, but half of the site already established as Airey, Cookson & Company is available for excavation, although it would be an exceedingly difficult project, with immense problems of disposal of spoilage and the shoring of a steep bank to the north side of the site. The other sides of

30 Plan of Airey, Cookson and Company
Glasshouse of Closegate, note particularly the position of the old town wall, which establishes the exact location of the site.
Central Library, Newcastle.
Photograph
Photo-Mayo

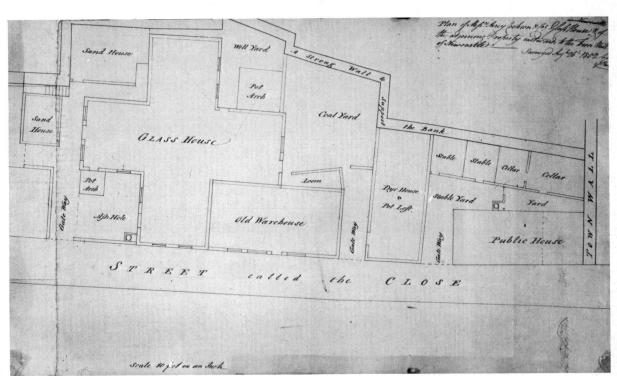

31 Wine glass
Round funnel bowl with
cut faceted stem. Normal
foot.
Height $5\frac{1}{2}$ in.
Decor: Group of fruit with
bird in white enamel.
Circa 1765
Victoria and Albert
Museum, London

Photograph
Photo-Mayo

32 Wine glass
With ogee bowl. The base
of the bowl is flare cut,
merging into a diamond cut
stem. The foot is cut,
displaying six panels, a
most unusual feature.
Height $5\frac{1}{4}$ in.
Decor: Funereal monument
in pastoral setting in green,
beige and violet enamels.

Circa 1770
Bridge Glassworks,
Newcastle upon Tyne
Photograph
Photo-Mayo

56

33 Glass and goblet
(a) *Wine glass* Round funnel
bowl with opaque twist
stem. Normal foot.
Height $6\frac{5}{8}$ in.
Decor: Probably by Mary
Beilby. Floral garland and
inscribed name *Elizth Smith*
in white enamel.
Circa 1765

(b) *Newcastle Light Baluster
goblet* Round funnel bowl
with light baluster stem.
Foot normal.
Height $7\frac{1}{4}$ in.
Decor: Fruiting vine in
white enamel with worn
thin gilt rim.
Circa 1765
Victoria and Albert
Museum, London

Photograph
Photo-Mayo

57

the Close, between the Airey, Cookson site and Skinnerburn could be excavated with the co-operation of the local authority and, perhaps, the interest and practical support of Newcastle University. There is no doubt in the author's mind that the area will reveal valuable information to contribute to the great story of Newcastle and English Glass.

The period of Newcastle Glass from 1728 to the close of the eighteenth century reveals that most of the great tradition of Newcastle Light Balusters came from this area. It is also virtually certain that the great variety of faceted stem glasses, with an immense range of air twist and opaque twist stemmed goblets also came from these glass houses.

Finally, in reviewing this area, it is virtually without doubt that William, Ralph and Mary Beilby were closely associated with all these glass houses during the period that their work was done, when they operated as freelance decorators under private and personal commissions from wealthy traders and the noble families of England. The picturesque walks from the Cathedral precincts of Amen Corner, through the narrow chares of old Newcastle, down the steep stone-built staircases which rejoice in the names of Castle Garth Stairs, Dog Leap Stairs and Breakneck Stairs, down to the Close, and the walk along the side of the river towards Closegate and the large conglomeration of glass houses there must have been a most enjoyable part of the day to day life of the family.

During this age of elegance in Newcastle Glass, the records show that vast quantities of glassware were sent all over the world, and particularly south in the flat bottomed keelboats loaded with coal to the Thames; and it would appear that the price of Newcastle Glass varied with the price of coal. Mr Leybourne, a London merchant, has said:

' That the price of Newcastle Glass is uncertain; for when coals are plentiful, glass is cheap; when coals are dear, Newcastle Glass is so likewise. Not that they want coals at Newcastle; but they have no other conveyance for it to London, and thus, the basic course of the establishment of the great glass industry on the Tyne and the availability of coal as a basic fuel, were also to control its price.' This interdependence is epitomized in the glass William Beilby decorated and which he inscribed with the words *and the coal trade*. Unfortunately, it was not possible to photograph this glass.

This great period of Newcastle Glass was recognized by most countries of the world. It was said to be of brilliantly clear metal, and to glisten and refract the light more than any other glass by any other makers. The Newcastle Light Balusters were highlights of this supreme elegance from the medieval town based on coal.

58

The Newcastle characteristics of the Light Baluster are easy to recognize with their tall slim stems. The bowls were mostly round funnel, gracefully merging into stems which centred around a baluster, sometimes inverted. The baluster frequently were ornately finished with 'dripping tears'. Around the baluster were arranged variations of knops, beads and collars, but always beautiful in balance and form.

Apart from Light Balusters the Newcastle glassmakers fashioned many of the air twist and opaque twist stems of the period. Distinctive goblets with 'bucket' bowls were made in Newcastle and perhaps the finest surviving example is the Fitzwilliam Royal Goblet (Plate 1). Ale glasses with deep bowls, wine glasses with ogee bowls, squat firing glasses, and slender ratafia glasses are all part of this unexpected 'era of elegance'.

A typical and attractive example of a Newcastle Light Baluster, decorated by William Beilby, is illustrated in full colour in plates 34 and 35.

The whiteness of the glass was achieved by fine technique in the use of decolouring agents and the vital high content of approximately 32 per cent lead oxide. This made the finished glass metal brilliant and 'soft' and thus very suitable for engraving and decorating.

There was a demand from overseas for glasses for decoration and famous Dutch engravers such as Jacob Sang, David Wolffe, Aert Schouman and Franz Greenwood decorated Newcastle glasses in this way.

Perhaps more important still was William Beilby, the master, with his exuberant brother Ralph and his pretty and shy sister Mary, who were to find in this glass a perfect medium for their art.

34 and 35 Newcastle Light Baluster goblet
Round funnel bowl with light baluster stem. Foot normal. Height $7\frac{1}{4}$ in.
Decor: By William Beilby and signed *Beilby pinxit*.
Front: Unidentified Arms, probably fictitious, in full colour enamels with scroll.

Reverse: Classical ruins and pyramid in pastoral setting in white enamel. Faint traces of gilt rim.
Circa 1765
Victoria and Albert Museum
Photograph
Photo-Mayo

60

9 A Beilby glass summary

Because not every Beilby glass was signed and dated, it is extremely difficult to assess with absolute certainty who, between William and Mary, decorated the range of glasses authenticated as Beilby.

We do know that when William returned from Birmingham to work in Newcastle in late 1760 he was approaching his twenty-first birthday while Mary was still a schoolgirl of eleven, so that during the experimental and formative period of William's work, Mary could not have assisted at all.

From this we can deduce that all the great early works like the Decanter of 1762 for the Common Council of Newcastle, the George III Royal Goblets of 1762 and the Standard of Hesleyside were, without any doubt, decorated by William Beilby. The confirming factor must, of course, be the signature on the Royal Goblet in the Fitzwilliam Museum (see plate 2).

From these early works the style is clearly established; it is very positive, with the unsurpassed delicacy of touch of a great artist.

From 1764, Mary was taught the art of glass painting by William and we find a greater variety of subjects. Mary never signed a single glass, so we are left with nothing but conjecture as to which works were done, or partly done, by her.

One factor which emerges is that many of the glasses decorated during this period were much simpler in style and there is a marked change in the strength of the brushwork. Some of the pieces have a considerably coarser style and these can, the author is convinced, be attributed to Mary.

Her early works were mostly small ogee bowl opaque stemmed glasses, decorated in white enamel with simple floral garlands, bee-hives with bees, and pastoral scenes. Barley and hops were decorated on deep bowled ale glasses.

William Beilby was particularly fond of the 'fruiting vine' motif and he used this in many forms as main decoration, often to support other basic designs.

Mary gained experience and confidence and extended her work to include the vine motif and also classical ruins. It is suggested by

61

the author that the following glasses, illustrated in this book, were the work of Mary – plates 24, 48, 50, 51, 58, 60, 81, 82, 83, 84(b) and 85.

In considering the presentation of a summary of the total works of William and Mary Beilby it is perhaps fortunate that we can place them in clear separate subject categories. The following Beilby Glass Summary is not presented in any order of significance or importance.

PLATE		DESCRIPTION	ATTRIBUTED TO	PAGE
		Heraldic		
1	s	The Fitzwilliam Royal Goblet (*Front*)	William	2
2	s	The Fitzwilliam Royal Goblet (*Reverse*)	William	2
3	s	The 'Pembroke' goblets	William	10
4		The 'Lowndes' goblet	William	14
10		The 'Horsey' wine glasses	William	23
52	s	The Philadelphia Royal Goblet (*Front*)	William	96
53	s	The Philadelphia Royal Goblet (*Reverse*)	William	97
54		The Rockingham goblet	William	100
55		The 'Turner' goblet (*Front*)	William	101
56		The 'Turner' goblet (*Reverse*)	William	101
57		The 'Buckmaster' goblet	William	104
61		The 'Van Dongen' goblet	William	109
69		The 'Thomas Vaughan' goblet (*Front*)	William	120
70		The 'Thomas Vaughan' goblet (*Reverse*)	William	121
72	SD	The Victoria and Albert bowl (*Front*)	William 1765	128
73	SD	The Victoria and Albert bowl (*Reverse*)	William 1765	128
74		The 'Margaret and Winneford' bowl (*Front*)	William	130
75		The 'Margaret and Winneford' bowl	William	131
76		The 'Margaret and Winneford' bowl (*Reverse*)	William	131
78	D	The Standard of Hesleyside goblet (*Front*)	William 1763	135
79	D	The Standard of Hesleyside goblet (*Reverse*)	William 1763	135
97	SD	The Newcastle decanter (*Reverse*)	William 1762	160
98	SD	The Newcastle decanter (*Front*)	William 1762	161
		Heraldic – presumed fictitious or unidentified		
6		Sloping shoulder decanter	William	19
26	s	The 'Truth and Loyalty' decanters	William	46
34	s	Wine glass (*Front*)	William	60
35	s	Wine glass (*Reverse*)	William	60
36		Wine glass (b)	William	64
38		Goblet (b)	William	67
41		Wine glass 'Pro Patria'	William	75
67		The 'Laing' decanter and glasses	William	116

s–Signed
D–Dated

63

64

PLATE	DESCRIPTION	ATTRIBUTED TO	PAGE
	Sporting scenes		
44	Wine glass (b)	William	84
	Inscribed		
33	Wine glass (a)	Mary	57
58 D	Tumbler (*Front*)	Mary 1767	105
59	Tumbler (*Reverse*)	Mary	105
64	The 'Clavering' goblet	William	113
65	Masonic firing glass	Mary and William	113
83	The 'Temperance' firing glass	Mary	143
	Scrolls (including floral garlands)		
9	Ratafia glass (b)	William	22
9	Wine glass (c)	William	22
24	Wine glass (b)	Mary	42
50	Ale glass	Mary	92
51	Wine glass (b)	Mary	93
82	Three wine glasses	Mary	142

D–Dated

36 Two glasses
(a) *Wine glass* Round funnel bowl, opaque spiral stem with rare blue inset corn. Foot normal. Height $6\frac{3}{4}$ in.
Decor: Fruiting vine in white enamel.
Circa 1765
(b) *Wine glass* Ogee bowl with fine mesh opaque twist spiral stem. Foot normal. Height 6 in.
Decor: Unidentified armorial figure in red and white enamel with the inscribed words *Pro Patria* in white.
Circa 1770
Fitzwilliam Museum, Cambridge
Photograph
Photo-Mayo

Observations on a Beilby Glass Summary

The attributing of the glass decorating to either William or Mary Beilby is purely an expression of opinion by the author after detailed and sustained examination of all the specimens, particularly observing the differences in brushwork technique.

The opinions of other persons connected with the glass departments of famous art establishments was also obtained and in general there was agreement that the 'attributed' conclusions arrived at in the Beilby Glass Summary were correct.

Although the range of Beilby glass studied and photographed in this publication is the most wide and comprehensive ever achieved, it is not considered by any means to be complete or even near completion. Certain private collectors would not accord co-operation in a study of their examples or permission to photograph and reproduce them.

Doubtless as the genius of the Beilbys becomes more widely recognized, more great specimens will be discovered.

Gilding

A number of Beilby glasses were gilded on the rims and it is perhaps to be regretted that this gilding was somewhat inexpertly done.

37 Wine glass
Bell bowl with opaque twist
stem. Normal foot.
Height $6\frac{1}{2}$ in.
Decor: Fruiting vine in
white enamel with gilt rim.
Circa 1765
Philadelphia Museum of
Art
Photograph
Alfred J. Wyatt

38 Two goblets
(a) *Goblet* Bucket bowl with
opaque spiral twist stem.
Foot normal.
Height $7\frac{3}{8}$ in.
Decor: Classical ruins with
standing figures and Beilby
butterfly in white enamel.
Circa 1770
(b) *Goblet* Round funnel bowl
with opaque spiral twist
stem in white. Foot normal
Height $7\frac{13}{16}$ in.
Decor: Unidentified arms
with the motto *Amor et
Amicitia* in white enamel.
Gilt rim.
Circa 1765
Victoria and Albert Museum
London
Photograph
Photo-Mayo

66

67

With modern gilt rimming, real gold is used in liquid bright gold form, but William employed a rather crude method with a medium of oil or varnish. The gilt was hand brushed around the rim and unfortunately most of it has perished over the years. Traces of the gilt rims, although well worn, can be seen on glasses shown in plates 78 and 81, while a very good example of a surviving gilt rim is clearly shown on the Royal Goblet in plates 52 and 53. Another very good example of a gilt rim is on the Van Dongen Goblet in Plate 61.

Enamel

Some of the early Beilby glasses are decorated with somewhat thin 'wash' enamel with little gloss, but the later firings show a positive white enamel gloss with almost a relief effect.

Most of the white enamelled Beilby glasses can be recognized by a distinctive bluish tint. In the Heraldic glasses of multi-coloured enamels, certain of the colours are exquisitely delicate, particularly the turquoise, which the author, over many years' glass study, has not seen reproduced in any modern glass.

The Beilby Butterfly

From a very early stage in his work of hand painting on glass, William Beilby had embodied almost as a signature the figure of a butterfly in most of his decor compositions. These butterflies are to be seen in all sorts of odd corners, on his glasses and the best examples are to be seen on plates 29 and 39

Beilby Dated Glasses

The Beilby family started their decorating of glassware about 1761 and probably finished in 1778. Certain works were dated and an even smaller number were signed. The full list of glasses illustrated in this book and dated is as follows:

1762 The fragmentary decanter, with the Arms of Newcastle upon Tyne and the Arms of Sir Edward Blackett, Mayor of Newcastle, dated 1762. Plates 97 and 98.

1762 The goblet, with the Royal Arms of George III and the Prince of Wales, signed by William Beilby. This goblet, although not actually dated, must be acknowledged as 1762, the year of the birth of the Prince of Wales. Plates 1 and 2.

1763 The goblet, 'The Standard of Hesleyside' dated 1763. Plates 78 and 79.

1764 The miniature air twist wine glass with vine motif, dated 1764. Plate 40.

68

1765   The $9\frac{7}{8}$ in. bowl, with Arms and scroll work, dated 1765. Plates 72 and 73.
1767   The inscribed tumbler, 'success to the Swordmakers' dated 1767. Plates 58 and 59.
1769   The inscribed flask, 'Thos. Brown', dated 1769. Plate 63.

Other dated glasses are known to be in existence, but owing to technical difficulties they are not illustrated in this book. Two examples are detailed as follows:

1764   Inscribed bowl of shallow circular shape with flared foot. Inscribed to JOHN and MARG.^{t} DIXON in white enamel, $4\frac{1}{2}$ in. diameter. Below the inscription HAWKWELL and dated 1764. On the reverse an oval medallion in a scroll, and dotted diaper design.
1764   Inscribed flask. A typical Newcastle flask of the period. The glass metal is of moderate quality and it is inscribed to MR. HUTCHINSON STONEY GILE and dated 1764.

39 Goblet
Bucket bowl with opaque
twist stem. Foot normal.
Height 7 in.
Decor: Fruiting vine with
tree and Beilby butterfly
in white enamel.
Circa 1765
Cecil Higgins Art Gallery
Photograph
Photo-Mayo

40 Wine glass
Round funnel bowl with
spiral opaque twist stem.
Foot normal.
Height $4\frac{1}{4}$ in.
Decor: Fruiting vine and
initials H.C. in white
enamel.
Dated 1764
Victoria and Albert Museum

Photograph
Photo-Mayo

70

10 Belated recognition

It is significant that in all early books on old English Glass, even by such famed authorities as Hartshorne and Bles, printed as recently as 1925, Beilby glass is illustrated yet not recognized as Beilby or Newcastle Glass. It would appear that the greatness of the Newcastle Light Baluster period and the important Beilby association of the late eighteenth century has been generally ignored, even by our own eminent early writers, presumably through lack of available research facilities.

Fortunately, later writers of glass literature such as Thorpe, Honey, Charleston and Elville have given deserved, if belated, recognition to the greatness of the Beilbys.

Part Two
11 The Beilby family

The Beilby story begins in Scarborough, Yorkshire on 12 March 1706, when William Beilby Senior was born. There was nothing outstanding in his antecedents, but his family were typical of the English middle-classes, eminently respectable and brought up in a strict Church of England background.

From an early age he had great artistic tendencies and was ultimately to work as a silversmith and jeweller. He was rich in artistic talent but completely failed to reap any financial rewards in his lifetime, which was a permanent struggle. He was not really a businessman and in Scarborough itself, he appears to have made very little impact.

In 1733, he courted and married Mary Bainbridge at St Margaret's Church in Durham City on 1 September. Mary Bainbridge was the perfect match for William Beilby – she was a cultured woman of great refinement and – most important – she had courage enough to sustain her struggling husband through very difficult times.

Few marriages can have been so blessed as this one, and from the union came a wonderful family of culture and artistic fulfilment, consisting of five boys and two girls.

John born in Durham City in May 1734
Richard born in May 1736
Elizabeth born in August 1738
William born in June 1740, who was to become the great William Beilby, the most famous decorator of glass of all time.
Ralph born in August 1743, who was to become the master of the great wood-engraver Thomas Bewick, and who was to be the real business head of the Beilby family.
Thomas born in December 1747
Mary born in February 1749. Sad and pathetic Mary, who was to suffer so much, both physically and mentally, and who was to establish her own niche in history as the collaborator and active assistant of her brother William in his great art of glass decorating.

After his marriage in 1733, William Beilby Senior decided to

72

settle down and establish a business in Durham City as a silversmith. He was to struggle hard for many years and this struggle was intensified as his family increased.

Although no record can be found of William Beilby Senior being a member of any of the City Liveries and Guilds, he achieved a reputation for sound work, and we find that in 1748 he executed a silver cup with gem ring for the Church of St Mary le Bow in Durham. In 1750 he made a silver tankard with domed cover for an unknown church in Durham City.

The most important aspect of the life of William Beilby Senior was that in spite of his immense financial difficulties, he was able to educate all his children adequately. They were a great credit both to him and to his wife Mary.

In his lifetime, Ralph, the energetic businessman, the engraver of seals and a doyen of the city of Newcastle upon Tyne, was to his father, perhaps, the greatest source of pride, but it was William, however, the superb artist and dreamer, the Latin scholar, who was to reach the real pinnacle of fame.

Failure

In Durham City, the struggles of William Beilby Senior reached their final stage when he failed in business. The strain had been enormous, but he had managed to educate his family. Richard and William had been sent to Birmingham to learn the art of seal engraving and enamelling. Ralph had stayed with his father to learn the art of a silversmith and jeweller, and was to become one of the most skilled engravers of silver and seals in the country.

The failure of the business must have been a profound shock to the entire family and they rallied around their father in no uncertain fashion. No record has yet been traced that William Beilby Senior went bankrupt, and it is assumed that as a craftsman he merely terminated his business and paid off his debts with the help of his family and friends. We find one happier note during this period in Durham City. In 1757 William Beilby Senior was witness, and signed the register, at the marriage of his friends Thomas Wilson of Hartlepool and Elizabeth Huggins of Stockton.

In 1759 the family moved to Gateshead, where it is recorded 'They were in dire straights'.

On this period, the comment of Thomas Bewick is the most revealing: 'This state of things could not have lasted very long for the industry, ingenuity and united energies of the family must soon have enabled them to soar above every obstacle.'

The short stay and work in Gateshead must have been the most trying period for the family. Even Mrs Mary Beilby helped materially

73

by teaching in Gateshead, whilst her daughter Mary taught drawing to young ladies in Newcastle.

For the family the real turning of the tide towards recovery came when Ralph and William decided to enter business on their own account in Newcastle, and this is described in fuller detail in the chapters devoted to William and Ralph Beilby.

By 1762 the family fortunes had handsomely recovered, but the long struggle had been too much for their father, for after a period of quiet retirement he died on 28 March 1765.

In his final days William Beilby Senior must have experienced some bitter moments in dwelling on his own failure, but he had consolation at the end. The family were solidly united and he was sustained by a wife of culture and understanding. He had the satisfaction of seeing his family all working in art forms. In his waking hours and declining years he could not have imagined that the Beilby family would live on in history and art to achieve a fame and immortality accorded to very few artists of world stature.

41 Wine glass
Ogee bowl with fine mesh
opaque twist stem.
Folded foot.
Height 6 in.
Decor: Unidentified
armorial crest in red and
white enamel, with the
inscription *Pro Patria* in
white enamel. *Circa* 1767.
Cecil Higgins Art Gallery,
Bedford, England
Photograph
Photo-Mayo

75

12 Ralph Beilby

In considering the story of the Beilby family, one is perplexed. Four main characters, all interlinked and interdependent like a finely woven tapestry.

With which of these characters to commence the story?

Undoubtedly the greatest emerging figure must be William, but for reasons of dramatic development the narrative can only start with Ralph Beilby, the real business brain of the family and from whom stems the glory of William and Mary, and without doubt the greatness of Thomas Bewick.

Ralph Beilby, the third son of William Beilby Senior, was born in Durham City on 12 August 1743. He was educated at Durham Grammar School, where he became a proficient classics and art scholar. One of his earlier accomplishments was that of music, and his wide interests made him very much a man about town.

As his elder brothers Richard and William were learning the arts of enamelling and painting in Birmingham, Ralph was left very much with the task of assisting his father as a silversmith and jeweller. He very quickly became highly skilled as an engraver in silver, and it is recorded in the Memoir of Thomas Bewick that 'what he excelled in was ornamented silver engraving. In this, as far as I am able to judge, he was one of the best in the Kingdom.' When his brother Richard returned from Birmingham, Ralph was quickly to learn from him the art of copper engraving and seal cutting.

The struggles of his father were to affect Ralph greatly and, realizing the business limitation of Durham City, he extended the sphere of his work to Gateshead and, of much greater importance, to Newcastle upon Tyne. He soon established a fine reputation as a seal cutter and considerably helped the family fortunes by his ingenuity and work.

When his father failed in Durham City in 1759, Ralph was the first to lead the move to Gateshead. His business brain was to establish him as the true leader of the family, and it was not long before he had made favourable impressions on many shrewd merchants in the great Northern metropolis across the river, New-

76

castle upon Tyne. His studies in seal cutting were to force him to give greater attention to the art of chivalry and heraldry. He became such an authority in heraldry that he was, from time to time, consulted by most of the noble families of the North Country. This knowledge of heraldry and his considerable skill as an engraver were to become important factors in the later development of his younger brother William and his great work on glass.

Although realizing the financial necessity, Ralph never accepted the fact of living in Gateshead, and it was typical of him that when an unexpected opportunity occurred, he seized it with both hands. The greater work of seal cutting and copper engraving in the North of England was almost entirely centred on the regional capital of Newcastle upon Tyne, and was a very closed shop. This was understandable, as clients were mainly banks and integrity was vital when there was the possibility of forgery of banknotes and documents.

There had developed in Newcastle a sensational criminal case unparalleled in Northern history. A well known engraver named Jameson was charged with committing a forgery on the Old Bank of Newcastle. (It is important to remember that at this time forgery was a capital crime and Jameson was being tried for his life.) The records show that Jameson was very close to being hanged, but when things looked at their blackest, a witness was produced who threw some element of doubt on the case. Because of insufficient evidence to convict him beyond reasonable doubt, the case was dismissed and Jameson was discharged. The character of Jameson had been damaged as a natural result of the case and his work virtually ceased. It was afterwards discovered that the witness produced at the late hour had committed perjury.

Amen Corner

It was here that Ralph Beilby stepped in and established himself in business very close to Jameson's old premises. This was at Amen Corner on the south east corner of the Cathedral Church of St Nicholas in the centre of the old city, and very close to the great Norman castle which gave Newcastle its name. Ralph called the business Beilby and Company and brought in his brothers Richard and William to help him (see plate 42).

A thriving and busy workshop was created and once again we must rely on the memoir of Thomas Bewick to give us a graphic description of the place and time:

'For such was the industry of my master that he refused nothing, coarse or fine. He undertook everything which he did in the best way he could. He fitted up and tempered his own tools, and adapted

77

them to every purpose, and taught me to do the same. This readiness brought him in an overflow of work, and the work-place was filled with the coarsest kind of steel stamps, pipe moulds, bottle moulds, brass clock faces, door plates, coffin plates, bookbinders letters and stamps, steel, silver, and gold seals, mourning rings &c. He also undertook the engraving of Arms, Crests and cyphers, or silver, and every kind of job from the silversmiths; also engraving bills of exchange, bank notes, invoices, account heads and cards. These last he executed as well as did most of the engravers of the time.'

Whilst these activities were going on, there came about another development which was of the greatest importance. Ralph Beilby's brother William, for whom he had the greatest affection, had become attracted to the great new art form which had now developed in Newcastle – the industry of glassmaking. Beautiful articles of glassware were being made very close to their premises at Amen Corner and it was not long before William was bringing to the workshop the most exquisite goblets of glass to be further decorated. William had experimented in many different ways in the hand painting of enamels on glass and he was to convey his keenness and enthusiasm to their younger sister, Mary. Mary was always closest to William, but Ralph was not slow to realize that his brother had discovered a new art form of the most far-reaching importance and he gave them every help and encouragement.

42 Amen Corner
At the corner of the churchyard of St Nicholas' Cathedral, where the workshop of Beilby and Company was established in 1760 and which was to become Bewick and Son in 1798.

78

The Brand Letters

Ralph Beilby's own work was to assume great importance, and he was commissioned by the historian John Brand to engrave Thornton's Monument Plate in his classic *History of Newcastle*. John Brand was so delighted with the excellence of this work that he became a life-long friend and associate of Ralph Beilby. Some indication of this friendship is to be found in the remarkable series of letters written by Brand to Ralph Beilby which were published by their mutual friend John Fenwick. They are a wonderful collection of personal anecdotes, giving an authentic impression of the times in which these fine characters lived.

Ralph Beilby also co-operated with Brand in the preparation and engraving of a plan of Newcastle upon Tyne in 1788. This plan is reproduced in plate 22. What is most interesting is that it clearly shows the sites of the Ouseburn and St Lawrence glass houses and which are marked High, Middle and Low Glass Houses. The repaired bridge over the Tyne is quite clear, whilst over to the left and east of the bridge we can see where the old city wall reaches the river at Closegate and where the famous flint glass houses of Dagnia, Airey and Cookson were situated.

Ralph Beilby had, by this time, taken up residence at the Forth Gardens, Newcastle, where he was joined later by William, Mary and other members of the family. Before the move from Gateshead, William Beilby Senior had died, and soon afterwards was followed by the eldest brother, Richard, after a long and distressing illness.

At Amen Corner, Ralph and William were to advance and consolidate their position in business and they at length looked towards the possibility of taking on an apprentice. They were not to know that their thoughts in this respect were to lead them to the most important meeting of their lives – one which was to become historic.

The Apprentice

They had discussed the question of apprenticeship with a very close friend, Mrs Simons, who was a Vicar's widow living in the beautiful Northumbrian village of Bywell, about eight miles west of Newcastle. Mrs Simons told the brothers that she thought she had found for them the ideal apprentice. She explained that she had a godson called Thomas, aged fourteen, who was apparently a magnificent and natural artist. He was always in trouble and somewhat unruly – drawing on gravestones, walls, anywhere – but what he sketched with all sorts of rude implements was a revelation. He appears to have been very much inclined towards nature and the countryside.

The Beilby brothers were so impressed with what they heard that they decided to drive over to Bywell and see for themselves this

79

young prodigy. When they arrived, noting with pleasure the lovely twin churches of the village, the brothers were received rapturously by Mrs Simons, who continued to give glowing accounts of her young godson and intimated that they were all to drive over to the cottage, named Cherryburn, near Mickley Bank, where the parents of young Thomas lived. The father received them courteously and tea was served.

After the usual pleasantries, the subject was brought around to that of young Thomas. His father was not at all complimentary about his young son and was quite frank in saying that he considered him undisciplined and rude tempered; but he was a 'likeable lad' who loved drawing and if that was what he wanted, then he was prepared to agree to the apprenticeship. He also explained that Thomas's grandmother had left him £20. 0. 0. for his proper apprenticeship and these funds would be made available.

The Preference

There remained the question of which one of the brothers Thomas would be indentured to. Thomas, an ungainly, gangling boy, was brought in and the brothers Beilby explained to him carefully something of their work of drawing, painting, enamelling and engraving and this appeared to please him very much.

He was then asked to choose which of the two masters he would care to be indentured to. Thomas looked carefully, and in his own words 'liking the look and deportment of Ralph the best, I gave the preference to him'. Arrangements were finally made for the apprenticeship to commence on 1 October 1767. And so, the young Thomas was apprenticed to Ralph Beilby at the age of fourteen.

There is no doubt that this significant and historic act completely overshadowed the life of Ralph Beilby in its fullness; for the name of this young boy was Thomas Bewick, who was to become the most famous engraver of wood in the world. It is hard to conjecture to what extent the lives of these two brothers were affected by their association with Thomas Bewick, for although Ralph was to be more closely connected with the day-to-day work of the young genius apprentice, it was perhaps William who was to benefit the most. Who can deny, after scrutinizing carefully the hand-painted masterpieces of William Beilby, that there was some little influence, perhaps even unconsciously, from Bewick, especially when we examine the pastoral scenes enamelled on the glasses and the little rural figures (see plates 60 and 63). Are they not very reminiscent of the masterful vignette woodcuts of Thomas Bewick? Whatever the contemplations, there is no doubt that this association of Thomas Bewick with the Beilbys very much enriched their lives; and it is to

80

43 Goblet
Large ogee bowl with
opaque twist stem. Normal
foot.
Height $7\frac{5}{8}$ in.
Decor: Fruiting vine with
tree in white enamel.
Beilby butterfly in white
(hidden on photo plate).
Circa 1765.
Victoria and Albert
Museum, London
Photograph
Photo-Mayo

81

their eternal credit that in the passing of two centuries, they emerge with enhanced stature.

Bewick Woodcuts

With the engaging of young Thomas Bewick as apprentice, Ralph Beilby was to extend and enlarge his own output. There is much controversy as to who taught Thomas Bewick the art of engraving wood. Ralph Beilby carried out much work for the well-known Dr Charles Hutton, who had seen woodcuts executed in London. Dr Hutton, after some initial difficulty, secured the correct type of boxwood and also the cutting implements. Ralph was not at all keen on this work, preferring to continue his basic love of engraving on copper. Thomas Bewick, however, immediately showed immense skill and a very handsome and lucrative business was built up.

During the apprenticeship years Ralph Beilby was to prove a strict taskmaster and was to impose a 'rigid code of discipline on the young Thomas'. At times Thomas would show some resentment at this, but he was always generous in his praise of the impartial fairness of his master. Ralph Beilby soon recognized the genius of his apprentice, and one of the most important and significant acts of encouragement was when he sponsored the entry of certain works of Thomas for the award of a grant from the Society of Arts in London. This society, now known as the Royal Society of Arts, made a grant of £7. 7. 0. and it was the first of many world-wide honours which were to come to Thomas Bewick.

Beilby and Bewick

On the termination of his apprenticeship, and after a short period of time which was spent in travel, he was taken into full partnership with Ralph Beilby in 1777, and the firm became known as Beilby and Bewick, still at Amen Corner.

Ralph Beilby has been so much overshadowed by the greatness of Thomas Bewick that one tends to overlook his own achievements. He must be remembered for his great engraving on copper for Thornton's Monument Plate in John Brand's *History of Newcastle*. John Brand himself described this as 'a work of great artistry and considerable skill'. Ralph Beilby also engraved the beautiful 'frontpiece' for *Gay's Fables* Newcastle, 1779. A beautiful surviving engraving of Bamburgh Castle, Northumberland is reproduced in plate 45. However, in writing of Ralph Beilby, one cannot move far from Thomas Bewick and there is no doubt that greatness was achieved by the collaboration between the two partners in the publication of certain of the great works of Thomas Bewick. The first of these was *A General History of Quadrupeds* in which Thomas Bewick was to display

82

his genius with the incomparable woodcuts of nature, whilst Ralph Beilby was to contribute the literary portion entirely. This classic was an immense success and in the lifetime of Thomas Bewick was to go to seven editions.

Friction
It is sad, however, to record that this very success was to cause trouble between the two partners. On the printing of the fourth edition some considerable difference arose between Thomas Bewick and Ralph Beilby as to the disposal of the copies. The resultant argument became so heated that ultimately an appeal was made to the public. Ralph Beilby eventually sold his share of the copyright to Thomas Bewick. This rift between Ralph Beilby and Thomas Bewick never properly healed and thereafter there was always a coldness between them.

Thomas Bewick and Ralph Beilby
Despite this, Thomas Bewick always referred afterwards to his master with some pride and respect. Perhaps the following extract from the *Memoir* tells a sad, reflective, but true to life, story and gives us the best insight into the complex minds of these great, but necessarily human, characters:
'I could not help thinking that he had suffered greediness to take possession of his mind; but, having promised to pay the sum, I made no further observations to anyone. On the other side of this account, I called to my remembrance the many obligations I owed him, for the wise admonitions he had given, and the example he had set me, while I was only a wild and giddy youth.

These I never could forget and they implanted so rooted a respect for him that I had grudged nothing I could not to promote his happiness. I had noticed, for some time past, that he had been led under a guidance and influence that made an alteration in his conduct for the worse; and he appeared to me not to be the Ralph Beilby he had been. I used to think him careful and sometimes penurious, and this disposition might indeed have crept and increased upon him; but whatever natural failings might be in his composition, these had heretofore been checked and regulated by the rules of morality and religion. It seemed to me that it must have been a maxim with him to do justice to all, but not to confer favours upon anyone; and yet he often joined me on conferring such, in various ways, upon our apprentices and others of our workpeople, for which we commonly had dirt thrown in our faces.

It does not require any great stretch of observation to discover that gratitude is a rare virtue, and that, whatever favours are conferred

83

84

upon an ungrateful man, he will conclude that these would not have been bestowed upon him had he not deserved them. In these our gifts, I was to blame in thus conferring favours that it would have been as well to let alone. In other charities he was not backward in contributing his mite, but in these matters he was led by wisdom. In the former case, mine, by giving vent to my feelings, were led by folly; but indeed, these follies were trivial compared with others relative to money matters, in which I had been led away by my feelings, in lending money to some, and in being bound for payment of it for others, which, if I had been more of his disposition, would not have happened; and I now clearly see and feel that, had it not been for these imprudences, I should, at this date, have found myself in better and very different circumstances than those I am in. My partner, indeed, often watched, and sometimes prevented me from engaging in such ruinous concerns, and would remark to me that it was impossible to serve any man who would not serve himself. As soon as Mr Beilby left me, I was obliged, from necessity, not choice, to commence author.'

Dissolution of Partnership

The partnership between Ralph Beilby and Thomas Bewick was dissolved on 6 January 1798, and Thomas Bewick continued at Amen Corner under the name of Thomas Bewick and Company. Thomas Bewick observes: 'After this, Mr Beilby gave up the engraving business and dedicated his whole time to the watch-crystal and clock manufactory, in which he had been long engaged before our separation.'

In 1778 had come the death of the mother, Mrs Beilby, and in 1780 Ralph Beilby married Ellen Hawthorne at St John's Church, Newcastle. The splitting up of the family from 1778 onwards was to cause the gradual withdrawal of Ralph Beilby from his artistic work, particularly after his marriage.

Ralph Beilby entered into a new partnership in business and in 1796 was joined by James Hawthorne, his brother-in-law. This business was quite successful at Dean Court, but in 1806 their premises were destroyed by fire and a new factory was built for the production of watch-glasses and clockwork. Soon after this was established, Ralph Beilby sought an early retirement.

He became a doyen of the arts, giving much encouragement to young artists and he also became quite an accomplished musician. Invitations to his sponsored musical evenings were much sought after. He became a founder member of the Literary and Philosophical Society of Newcastle upon Tyne, which has been nationally admired and recognized for two hundred years, and is still flourishing.

44 Three wine glasses
a) Ogee bowl with opaque twist stem.
Height $5\frac{7}{8}$ in.
Decor: Hunting scene in white enamel. Part of a set decorated with various sporting subjects.
b) Ogee bowl with opaque twist stem.
Height $5\frac{3}{4}$ in.
Decor: Exotic bird in pastoral setting. White enamel. Traces of gilt rim.
c) Ogee bowl with opaque twist stem.
Height $5\frac{7}{8}$ in.
Decor: Pyramid in pastoral scene in white enamel with gilt rim.
Circa 1765.
Lymbery Collection
Photograph
Photo-Mayo

45 Bamburgh Castle Northumberland in 1778
One of the few engravings confirmed to Ralph Beilby, found and available for reproduction.

85

On 4 January 1817, Ralph Beilby died, and was buried with considerable pomp and honour in the old Newcastle churchyard of St Andrew's; and today you can see the tombstone to his memory which is inscribed as follows:

'The buriel place of Ralph Beilby, gent, who departed this life January 4th 1817 aged 73 years. Also Ellen Beilby, who departed this life 20th November 1833 aged 78 years, the beloved wife of the above mentioned Ralph Beilby. Also of Mary Beilby, mother of the above Ralph Beilby, who died 18th June 1778 aged 66. M.I. St. Andrews.'

Postscript

There remains a final postscript to the death and burial of Ralph Beilby. Of the three principal Beilby characters in this book, William, Ralph and Mary, the author has only been successful in tracing the last will and testament of Ralph Beilby. It is an orthodox will leaving everything to his wife Ellen Beilby. It does, however, give us an authentic signature of Ralph Beilby, which is reproduced for the first time by kind permission of the University of Durham.

' Witnefs whereof I have hereunto set my hand and seal the twenty-fifth day of November in the year of our Lord one thousand, eight hundred and sixteen'

Ralph Beilby's signature

The real postscript comes in a letter which is also published for the first time by kind permission of the Literary and Philosophical Society of Newcastle upon Tyne. This letter, which is not clear enough for facsimile reproduction, is from the widow of Ralph Beilby to the Reverend A. Hedley. Apparently the Reverend A. Hedley had published certain statements made by Ralph Beilby's great friend and benefactor, Dr Hutton, concerning the work of Ralph and his family. She did not agree with certain aspects of what Dr Hutton had written and most certainly, her letter gives food for further thought and study, especially the reference to 'Perthshire' (see also pages 125 and 126).

86

COPY OF LETTER FROM MRS BEILBY TO REV. A. HEDLEY
Dated 28 December 1822.

Dear Sir,

I return you Doctor Hutton's letter with my thanks, and I cannot forebear expressing my surprise at Doctor Hutton's statement should be so erroneous in many points. In respect to what related to his own transactions with the persons he names, I daresay he was perfectly correct. When the Beilby's were young men the Doctor was intimate with them, particularly Mr. William, who some years kept an academy at Battersea. He left it not from its not being successful but from marrying a lady of large fortune 25 years younger than himself and resided with her in Perthshire more than 20 years. He never was near Nottingham. He had two sons and one daughter and a very few years ago he removed to Hull where he died within the last 2 years. Mrs. Beilby is lately dead. In respect to my husband, he had no concern in the engraving . . . whatever for over 20 years of his death and for the past 10 years not even in any commercial concern. Those . . . are indeed of little importance . . . and wishes to see any species of biography correct.

I send you some little things of Mr. Beilby's engraving, which I request you accept from me. I have not included Bamburgh Castle (plate 45) as the best thing he did but, bearing his own signature which I concluded you might like. The other . . . was the last thing he ever did . . . recently, to amuse himself and . . . me.

Yours truly,
E. M. Beilby

The final twist is in the last paragraph: 'The last thing he ever did . . . recently, to amuse himself and . . . me' was the engraving of his own tombstone (see plate 46).

46 Etching of Ralph Beilby's tombstone

13 William Beilby

So little is known of this supreme artist in glass that it is very difficult to do justice to his standing in the world of art and of glass by telling his life story. He was born on 9 July 1740, a time when printing and the written word was still very limited. It was also a time when records of births, marriages and deaths were not compulsory and thus we are presented with many gaps in his history.

Many of the facts known about William Beilby have been gleaned by intensive research and often by cross reference and circumstantial evidence from many persons, local authorities and letters. The author has been to Gateshead, Durham City, Hull, Battersea, Perth, Fife and Birmingham and searched through countless records, parish registers and commercial transactions of the period from William Beilby's birth until his death, but we still do not know where he lived and worked after leaving Newcastle upon Tyne – we still do not know where in Fife he was supposed to have helped manage an estate – we still do not know of the Battersea Academy where he was supposed to have been Master – we still do not know where and when he actually died and where he was buried.

Recently, when the author was in the United States, a discussion arose concerning William Beilby and whether any move could be made to acquire some of his finer pieces for a very famous museum. This museum thought, incorrectly perhaps, that the author had special knowledge of where these pieces could be found and at what price they could be obtained. The upshot of the discussion was that the Curator suggested the payment of up to four hundred thousand American dollars (that is to say over one hundred thousand pounds) to buy three or four Royal pieces of Beilby glass. Needless to say, they were quite unsuccessful in their offer, for these rare Beilby pieces are virtually priceless and unobtainable.

William Beilby, like his brothers, was educated at the grammar school in Durham City and was admitted in 1751 as a King's Scholar. Reports indicate that he proved to be a very good classics scholar and had an excellent command of Latin. This is reflected in many of William Beilby's signed works which have the Latin abbreviation of *invt* and *pinxt* after the signature.

88

47 Four exquisitely matched wine glasses
Trumpet bowl with drawn opaque fine mesh twist stem. Foot normal.
Height $6\frac{1}{4}$ in.
Decor: Fruiting vine in white enamel and gilt rim.
Circa 1770.
The Wyatt Collection
Photograph
Photo-Mayo

48 Two ale glasses
Elongated conical bowls with opaque twist stems. Foot normal.
Decor: a) Beehive with bees and scroll in white enamel.
Height 7 in.
b) Hops and barley in white enamel.
Height $7\frac{1}{8}$ in.
Circa 1765.
Victoria and Albert Museum, London
Photograph
Photo-Mayo

89

Because of the family financial difficulties, he was sent to Birmingham to learn the art and technical processes of enamelling in the July of 1751. Practically nothing is known of William's apprentice days in Birmingham, excepting that he learned the art of drawing and of enamelling at Bilston, near Birmingham, and was indentured to John Hezeldine, an enameller, on 3 July 1755, with a paid premium of £10. Most of the enamelling was carried out on metals like brass and copper, and he was to acquire particularly great skill in the preparation, mixing and grinding of the colour pigments. He was also to learn how to fuse and fire these pigments so that they were firm and highly glossed on the metal.

During his stay in Birmingham he lived frugally with his elder brother Richard, and apparently very much fretted to return to his native north country. One important point emerges from his Birmingham period, and that was that he apparently met many Stourbridge glassmakers, and this significant event turned his attention towards glass as an art medium.

William Beilby was a much quieter and reserved person than his brother Ralph, and this is possibly why we have so little knowledge of him. He was shy and self-effacing, but warmed when talking about painting and art. He was also sensitive to criticism and during his early efforts on glass, deliberately smashed many of the specimens he worked on because he was unhappy with the quality.

Return to the North

Like all members of the family, he had a great sense of loyalty and obligation and when he heard of the great financial difficulties his father was in, he decided to return to the North. He arrived back in Gateshead during late 1760, and was shocked to find that his mother had opened a school in Gateshead and was teaching there with the help of his younger sister Mary. With a tremendous will he set to work with his brother Ralph, and with the acquisition of the workshop at Amen Corner, quickly settled in to make his mark as an artist and a practical worker.

William Beilby loved the old town of Newcastle and was deeply sensitive to its medieval atmosphere. He loved to walk through the picturesque chares and gates and to make his way down the many stairs leading to the river. Alongside these stairs were many tradesmen working from tiny shops and frequently the work was carried out in the open air. There were the clogmakers, the tailors, the candlemakers (see plate 49). The steps were very busy with all manner of people moving up and down to the fashionable Close. At that time, most of the gentry lived in the Close, including Sir Walter Blackett, the Mayor of the town at the Mansion House. The noise of the

90

49 Old Staircase Castle Garth

50 Ale glass
Long straight sided funnel
bowl with opaque twist
spiral stem. Foot normal.
Height $7\frac{1}{4}$ in.
Decor: Geometric and
scroll design in white
enamel. Worn gilt rim.
Probably by Mary Beilby.
Circa 1765.
Cecil Higgins Art Gallery,
Bedford, England
Photograph
Photo-Mayo

**51 Two contrasting
glasses**
(a) *Firing glass*. Ogee bowl
with heavy opaque twist
stem.
Height $4\frac{1}{2}$ in.
Decor: Fruiting Vine and
tree with Beilby Butterfly
in white enamel. Foot,
heavy, terraced.
Circa 1765.
(b) *Wine glass*. Round
funnel bowl with light
opaque twist stem. Foot
normal.
Height 6 in.
Decor: Floral garland in
white enamel, almost
certainly executed by Mary
Beilby.
Circa 1765.
The Wyatt Collection
Photograph
Photo-Mayo

92

93

street criers and the picturesque characters of Newcastle made a lively scene. Newcastle traders were well-known for their ready wit and humour, and William Beilby loved walking down his favourite steps, ominously called Breakneck Stairs. He often took with him his younger sister Mary, and at the foot of the steps, which were very steep indeed, he would call on the glassmakers. He was very popular with the glassmakers, for they had a sense of feeling for a great artist.

The Closegate

William Beilby was tremendously impressed by the magnificence of the work turned out by the Closegate flint glasshouses and he was to meet a young expert in furnace construction, the son of John Williams. He had the conviction that he could fire enamels on to the surface of glass goblets and other glass shapes and that this would open up a completely new vista in glassmaking. With the co-operation of the furnace makers he began a series of experiments.

William had learned the art of hand mixing of enamel pigments in Birmingham and with infinite patience he ground these to a fine powder. This was a laboriously done by hand with a conventional pestle and mortar. When the required fineness had been reached, the enamels were washed and screened many times through the finest of hair filters. By this time, they had reached a consistency similar to fine mud and William, by persistent trial and error, then found the true secret. He introduced into the fine pigment a metallic flux and this, for the first time in the recorded history of glass, was to achieve a fusing of the colour enamel pigments into the brilliant clear transparent surface of the glass. By any standards this technical advance was magnificent, but when one considers that William Beilby worked in the confined space of a coal-fired furnace with all the problems of absence of temperature control and 'glass blooming' through fumes, his achievement can be regarded almost as a miracle.

With the help of the Closegate furnace makers he designed a special muffle extension to the furnace and by clever ventilation, veered the colour-destroying fumes away from the glass.

The critical temperature for firing enamel into flint glass depends on the volume of lead we have in the glass itself. With a full lead crystal lead oxide content of about 31 per cent, the glass metal would be 'soft' and the temperature has to be kept low (to about 520 degrees Centigrade). The temperature has to be brought as near to melting point as possible without collapse.

The margin against failure is very fine, no more than about 15 degrees. If it is too low the enamels will be underfired and will flake or rub off – if it is too high the glass will start to melt and collapse.

In modern glassworks we have electrified muffle furnaces with

94

precise gauges and automatic temperature control. The fumes are taken care of by the automatic opening and closing of built-in extractors. William Beilby had none of these – he had a coal-fired muffle and 'controlled' his temperature by the placing of the glass and the 'feel' of the heat on his cheeks and hands. His first efforts were with simple weak wash enamels in white. Specimens of this phase are shown in plates 7, 31 and 48. He achieved full fusing but the enamel was thin. Later, he was to make his enamels much more positive and dense, and the result was much better, with a fine gloss showing clearly on the enamel. This phase is illustrated on the fruiting vine glasses in plates 13, 33, 36 and 47. In 1761, he was able to fire multi-colours into glasses for the first time. The fusing was brilliant and wonderfully balanced in colour. Then, at last, he was able to concentrate on his great artistic ability in hand painting. His brush work, beautifully sensitive, yet with an absolute certainty of touch, was superb but perhaps the greatest feature was the perfect artistic balance achieved.

Heraldic Success

As news of his success spread around the glass houses, commissions and work were to come to William Beilby. He was given immense help by his younger brother Ralph, who had a great knowledge of heraldic designs and it is almost certain that some of the Beilby glasses have a touch of the work of Ralph, particularly some of the inscriptions, both plain printed and gothic. A reference to certain glasses, like the 'Pro Patria' in plate 41, plainly shows a marked similarity to the engraved print by Ralph Beilby on the authenticated drawing of the Ruined Tyne Bridge of 1771 (plate 62).

Between 1761 and 1763 many beautiful glasses were decorated in colour by William Beilby. It has been recorded that his first authentic and dated work was the 'Standard of Hesleyside' in 1763, but the author has discovered that this is not quite correct.

The first dated work was a decanter commissioned by the Common Council of Newcastle upon Tyne for the prospective Mayor, Sir Edward Blackett. This fine decanter, decorated by William Beilby, in full colour, is illustrated in plates 97 and 98. The front is beautifully decorated with the full arms of Newcastle upon Tyne in a rococo scroll with the signature *Beilby Junr pinxit & inv^t N'Castle 1762*. The reverse has the Arms of Sir Edward Blackett with a motif, which was to become a familiar feature of William Beilby's work, the fruiting vine below the word *Claret*.

There is a mystery surrounding this particular commission. Although the decanter was undoubtedly made in the Closegate glass house of Williams and Company and decorated by William Beilby

95

52 and 53 A Royal Goblet of George III
Located at the Philadelphia Museum of Art in the United States, this superb goblet, height $9\frac{1}{4}$ in., is similar in specification to its companion goblet on display at the Fitzwilliam Museum in Cambridge, England, and which is illustrated in plates 1 and 2. Careful study of the plates will reveal interesting differences in execution. Each goblet has its own artistic individuality.
Photograph
Alfred J. Wyatt

96

in 1762, the fact remains that Sir Edward Blackett did not become Mayor of Newcastle upon Tyne until 1764. Was it carried out 'in anticipation'? An interesting recent discovery by the author has revealed that a payment was made, and is recorded in the 'Disboursements of the Newcastle Common Council of Xmas 1764', of £7. 10. 0. to 'Onesiphorus Dagnia III Glafsmaker'. It must be presumed that the payment was for this actual decanter, and that as late as 1764 the Dagnias may well have still been directly connected with the early work of the Beilby family.

William Beilby's technique improved as he gained experience, and although most of his work showed exquisite brushwork with enamel, he frequently used a fine needle for the ultra-fine definition of the leaves and foliage in his pastoral designs.

William and Mary

By the latter part of 1762, William had taught something of the art of glass painting to his young sister Mary, who was then only thirteen years old, and from this time some of the Beilby glasses must be attributed to her. There is no doubt that William was very fond of his sister and there is considerable evidence to show that they worked together a tremendous amount in perfect harmony.

It is difficult to separate without doubt certain of the Beilby glasses decorated during this period and throughout their association, but William's work has a very clear and positive style. As far as the author can ascertain Mary apparently concentrated on designs in white, and her glasses are mostly decorated with floral garlands, simple pastoral scenes and particular vine, hop and barley patterns.

The Royal Goblets

In 1762 William Beilby carried out what was probably to be his most famous work, The Royal Goblets of George III. No one can find how these glasses were commissioned and paid for, but it would appear that on the birth of the Prince of Wales to George III on 4 August 1762, four or more Royal Glasses were commissioned. They were undoubtedly made in the Closegate glass house of Williams and Company, and decorated by William Beilby. They are beautiful, elegant goblets with bucket bowl, opaque stem and plain foot. In the superb decoration of these goblets, William Beilby established himself, at the age of twenty-two, as one of the greatest glass decorators of all time. Apart from one in private ownership, these three goblets are at present located as follows:

The Fitzwilliam Museum, Cambridge (plates 1 and 2).
The Philadelphia Museum, U.S.A. (plates 52 and 53).
Victoria and Albert Museum, London (bowl only).

98

The Fitzwilliam Museum specimen is reproduced in plate 1 with the Royal Arms, whilst the reverse, with the Arms of the Prince of Wales, is illustrated inside front in plate 2. Not all these goblets are signed, but the Fitzwilliam specimen is signed *WBeilby Junr NCastle invt & pinxt*. A careful study of the two plates is revealing and most rewarding. Observe particularly the exquisite brushwork on the Royal Arms and the superb scroll. The balance in tone of the full colour range is astonishing, especially when one considers a photograph of the goblet more than two hundred years old.

The Heraldic Group

The decorating of the Royal Goblets must have caused immense interest and enthusiasm amongst the glassmakers of Newcastle, and undoubtedly stimulated great attention from noble families in England and overseas. Commissions from the gentry poured in, and it established what is now known as the 'Heraldic' phase of William Beilby's work.

Under the Heraldic Group were many famous families. The most interesting of these, without question, was the Charlton family, with 'The Standard of Hesleyside', which is covered by a special chapter on pages 132 to 137.

Heraldic glasses covered in this book are as follows:

The Earl of Rockingham (page 100, plate 54).

Thomas Vaughan of Dorset (pages 120 and 121, plates 69 and 70).

Turner of Kirkleatham (page 101, plates 55 and 56).

Buckmaster of Lincoln, Northamptonshire and Devonshire (page 104, plate 57).

The Earl of Pembroke and Montgomery (page 10, plate 3).

The Lowndes Family (page 14, plate 4).

Van Dongen of Zeeland (page 109, plate 61).

The Charltons of Hesleyside (pages 134 to 138, plates 78 and 79).

There were of course others.

Most of this great work was carried out at the small workshop at Amen Corner. Although they were very much associated with the glassmakers at Closegate, the Beilby family worked as freelance agents and were not directly employed by any of the glass houses. They collected the various glasses from the glass houses, worked on them at Amen Corner, and when the decor was ready, the glasses were returned to the glass houses for firing.

It can, perhaps, be assumed that because of the volume of work the family must have been fairly well off by this time, but sadly enough this was not so. The responsibility of the family finances now rested on the shoulders of William and Ralph Beilby, and because of dire necessity they frequently accepted work and commissions of a lesser

99

54 The Rockingham Goblet

Bucket bowl with opaque twist stem. Foot normal.
Height $8\frac{7}{8}$ in.
Decor: The Arms of the Earl of Rockingham in full colour enamel with gilt rim.
Circa 1770.
Fitzwilliam Museum
Photograph
Photo-Mayo

55 and 56 The Turner Goblet
Bucket bowl with opaque twist stem. Folded foot. Height 7½ in.
Decor: (a) Front. The Arms of Turner of Kirkleatham in full colour enamel. (b) Reverse. Scene of classical ruins. Gilt rim worn. This goblet is one of the few Beilby glasses which show considerable signs of deterioration in the enamels. This could have been caused by exposure at some time.
Circa 1770.
Cecil Higgins Art Gallery
Photograph
Photo-Mayo

artistic nature, such as illustrated books, calendars and anniversary testimonials.

'Fictitious' Glass

Attracted to the Beilbys because of their outstanding work were merchant families who, while not entitled to bear Arms, nevertheless aspired to family Arms or Crests. It is presumed that Ralph Beilby had a very considerable hand in this, and, as a result, a number of glasses were decorated with so-called fictitious Arms.

The best example of this kind is the lovely Newcastle Light Baluster goblet decorated with a fictitious Coat of Arms, with a beautifully balanced setting of classical ruins on the reverse. This is illustrated on page 60, plates 34 and 35. This outstanding specimen of the work of William Beilby is signed, and it is perhaps amusing to reflect that whoever commissioned this 'phony' glass could hardly have realized that two hundred years later it would undoubtedly fetch a sum in excess of £1000 if it was sold at Sotheby's.

The following further unidentified Arms are illustrated in this book:

The Pro Patria ogee bowl glass (pages 64 and 75, plates 36(b) and 41).

The round funnel goblet with Arms and motto *Amor et Amicitia* (page 67, plate 38(b)).

The Truth and Loyalty decanters with unidentified Arms (page 46, plate 26).

The Laing decanter and two wine glasses, with scroll, fruiting vine and Beilby butterfly (page 116, plate 67), and once again it must be recorded that there may well be many others.

From 1762 to 1765 William and Mary were fully employed in decorating glass, and amongst the known, dated pieces during this period are the air twist miniature wine glass, dated 1764 (page 70, plate 40) and a lovely small inscribed bowl for the marriage of John and Margaret Dixon in the village of Hawkwell in Northumberland, inscribed and dated 1764. In 1765 William painted his greatest work, the crystal bowl described in detail on page 129, plates 72 and 73, and in the same year he completed a companion to this bowl, only recently discovered, the Margaret and Winneford bowl to commemorate the launching of the ship of the same name on the River Tyne (plates 74 to 76).

In this year of 1765 the family suffered a sad bereavement in the death of their much loved father, William Beilby Senior, in Gateshead. The funeral took place at the Cathedral Church of St Nicholas and in the churchyard very close to Amen Corner where his brilliant family worked so hard and so well, he was laid to rest.

The death of their father brought about many inevitable changes.

102

To their house at Forth Banks, very close to the glass houses, they brought their widowed mother, and there the two brothers, William and Ralph and their young sister Mary, lived through a decade of achievement and sadness. Ralph had now become the true head of the family; William had assumed a more gentle and accommodating rôle. He had always been deeply religious and he was much respected by his family, friends and fellow workers. Thomas Airey, whose family had considerable financial interests in the glass houses, was a close friend of William, and the two were very much associated with works of charity. Thomas Airey became treasurer to the Newcastle 'Lunatick' Hospital and frequently called upon William to help, which he gladly did.

William made it his business to look after Mary; her health was not good and she was very shy and retiring. Although Ralph was a man of the world and well known to everyone, it was William to whom Mary turned. They frequently explored together the narrow chares and stairs and battlements of the walled medieval city of Newcastle. At this period, the family were still in some financial difficulty and old Mrs Beilby continued to teach in Gateshead.

The year 1767 was to be truly momentous for all the family.

William and Ralph had decided to move to the Close, nearer to the glass houses, and, because of the continuing financial struggle, William decided to begin teaching drawing. On 14 February 1767, the following advertisement appeared in the *Newcastle Journal*: 'DRAWING. William Beilby proposes teaching young ladies and gentlemen in the several branches of the art of drawing, at his house in the Close, Newcastle upon Tyne.'

But something of much greater importance was to happen to all of them, although they were not to realize it at the time. The day came when the two brothers made their historic drive to Bywell to find a new apprentice, whose name was Thomas Bewick, described in the chapter devoted to Ralph Beilby. The young Thomas first lived with the Beilbys at Forth Banks, but later it is assumed he moved with them to the Close.

The Swordmakers
There is no doubt that Thomas Bewick not only very much interested himself in the work of his new master Ralph, but also in the more artistic work on glass by William. In actual fact, we can see a very clear connection. In the *Memoir of Thomas Bewick*, written some years later, Thomas writes: 'The first job I was put to was blocking out wood and etching sword blades for William and Nicholas Oley, Sword Manufacturers etc., of Shotley Bridge.'

In the same year of the apprenticeship of Thomas Bewick, a

103

57 The Buckmaster Goblet

Bucket bowl with opaque twist stem and folded foot. Height 7 in.

Decor: The Arms of Buckmaster of Lincoln, Northamptonshire and Devonshire, in full colour enamel with supporting rococo scroll. Gilt rim.

On reverse, fruiting vine in white enamel.

Circa 1765.

After two hundred years, the enamel decoration on this goblet is in perfect condition and particular notice should be made of the exquisite light heliotrope of the scroll and the very positive colours of the red and blue in the Arms. Altogether a magnificent piece, undoubtedly by William Beilby, and displayed in the lovely setting of the Cecil Higgins Art Gallery in Bedford, England

Photograph
Photo-Mayo

104

58 and 59 Tumbler
Conical shape in flint glass
Height $4\frac{1}{2}$ in.
Decor: The initials WOA
and rococo scroll in white
enamel. Dated 1767. On
reverse inscribed *Success to
the Swordmakers*. This
tumbler is important in that
it clearly established the
link between William and
Ralph Beilby and the
apprentice Thomas Bewick
in their work of glass
decorating. (In his *Memoir*,
Thomas Bewick refers to his
early work for the sword-
makers Oley of Shotley
Bridge.)

Wilkinson Sword Company
Ltd., England
Photograph
Photo-Mayo

special tumbler was decorated for the swordmakers of Shotley Bridge (page 105, plates 58 and 59). This tumbler is not outstanding in itself, but it clearly is the work of Mary Beilby. It is $4\frac{1}{2}$ in. high, and is decorated in white enamel, with the initials W^OA in a rococo scroll whilst on the reverse side is inscribed *Success to the Swordmakers*. The initials are W.O. for William Oley, while his wife Ann has the single initial, common practice in this period.

And so the young genius Thomas Bewick came to live with the Beilbys. The household then comprised of Ralph, William, Mary and the old lady, Mrs Beilby. It was, on the whole, a strictly-run household with formal church attendance by the family each Sunday.

When young Thomas found himself at the wrong end of a fight with three apprentices in the Close, he was immediately disciplined and was obliged to attend his master to church twice a day every Sunday, and at night-time had to read the Bible to old Mrs Beilby and her shy, but attractive, daughter Mary.

There is no doubt that from a very early period of his apprenticeship, Thomas Bewick was attracted to Mary. Mary was then eighteen and Thomas fourteen, so it is hard to assess who influenced whom. Mary had already received a period of instruction in drawing from William and her other brother Thomas, who was a drawing master, but Thomas Bewick, even at that early age, was a very strong character and his will in the end must have prevailed.

This is perhaps an interesting conjecture, and it is possible that certain of Mary's work on glass had a marked 'Bewick' influence. Study the similarity in styles between the pastoral scene ogee glass in plate 60 which is presumed to have been done by Mary Beilby, and the vignettes executed by Thomas Bewick, plates 90 and 92.

Consider also the fact that William Beilby ran a drawing school continuously from 1767 until 1778, when his final advertisement appeared in the *Newcastle Journal* of 3 October 1778:
'Drawing Academy. Mr. Beilby returns thanks for favours received from his patrons during the continuance of his drawing school, and desires to inform them that he proposes an exhibition of the drawings and paintings of his pupils at his house in Northumberland Street, Newcastle.'

In many respects, the young Thomas Bewick was fortunate that he had entered a family that was so artistically industrious, so cultured and so understanding of his early difficulties, for he was an impetuous and sometimes intractable youth. As the years passed, William Beilby was to continue his great work on glass. There is a happy note in 1768, when William and his brother Ralph attended the wedding of the daughter of Christopher Dagnia. It is recorded in the *Newcastle Courant* of 30 July 1768: 'Ensign Holmes of General

106

Brudenal's Regiment and Miss Dagnia a daughter of Mr. Christopher Dagnia, a considerable glass owner of this town, married at St John's. An amiable young lady with a considerable fortune.'
Another interesting link between the Dynasty of Dagnia and the Beilbys.

In 1769, Thomas Beilby left the family to open a drawing school in Leeds, and his advertisement appears as follows:
Leeds Mercury, 24 October 1769. 'Mr. T. Beilby from Newcastle upon Tyne proposes opening a drawing school in a commodious room to initiate young ladies and gentlemen into a knowledge of the polite and useful accomplishment. Enquire at Mr. Grimshaw's Academy.'

In 1770 a most important partnership agreement entered into was concerning the leading flint glass house at Closegate in Newcastle. The details of this partnership have recently been found by the author and are appended herewith for the first time:

'31st January 1770.
Article of co-partnership.
PARTIES: 1 John Cookson of Whitehill, Co. Durham.
        2 Thomas Airey of Newcastle upon Tyne.
        3 Joseph Wilson (gent) of Newcastle upon Tyne.
        4 George Dickinson (gent) of Newcastle upon Tyne.
21 year partnership in a flint glass or white glass ware business at the glass house at the Closegate in Newcastle upon Tyne. Joint Stock £72000. 1) 15/30. 2) 9/30. 3) 4/30. 4) 2.30.'

Extract from article: 'Partners and joint traders in employment trade or business of making flint glass or white glass wares at the glass works at the Closegate in Newcastle.'

Signed and sealed by all four.
The important point about this partnership is that it establishes one of the main glass houses used by William Beilby in his decorating of glass because of his close friendship with Thomas Airey. This was the glass house converted from the Dissenters' Meeting House at the Closegate, the plan of which is illustrated on page 55, plate 30.

A vital point is recorded by The Surtees Society. In 1770, John Cookson and Thomas Airey were Protestant Dissenters.

Also in 1770, in collaboration with Charles Hutton the historian, a new plan of Newcastle upon Tyne was engraved by Ralph Beilby, in which there was this comment:
' amongst sixteen glaſs houses in production two glaſsworks for Flint and White Glaſs.' One of these was the 'Dissenters' Glass house' at Closegate, described above, and the other was John Williams and Company, further along the Close towards Skinnerburn.

107

60 Wine glass
Large ogee bowl with short
opaque twist stem. Foot
normal.
Height $6\frac{1}{2}$ in.
Decor: Pastoral scene with
shepherd and sheep in
white enamel. Worn gilt
rim.
Circa 1765.
Fitzwilliam Museum,
Cambridge
Photograph
Photo-Mayo

61 The Van Dongen Goblet
Round funnel bowl with opaque twist stem. Foot normal.
Height $9\frac{1}{4}$ in.
Decor: The Arms of Van Dongen of Zeeland in full colour enamels within a cartouche surmounted by a coronet. The Arms are supported with foliage, trees and a floral garland in white. Excellent gilt rim.
Circa 1765.
Pilkington Glass Museum, St Helens, England
Photograph
Photo-Mayo

109

A West View of the Rui[n]

This Bridge has stood above 500 Years, for according to Matt. Paris, the former Bridge w[ch] wa[s] wood, was burnt in the Year 1248, together with a great part of the Town. After this Misfortune, the [Bi]shop of Durham granted Indulgences to all who would assist in Rebuilding it. Several other [Pre]lates also granted Indulgences for the same Purpose. By w[ch] means it was compleated

VIEW OF THE OLD TYNE BRIDGE drawn by WILLIAM, and engraved by his br[other]

62 Panorama of a West view of the ruins of Newcastle Bridge

110

R. Beilby Sculp.

NEWCASTLE BRIDGE.

d till the late dreadful Flood on the 17th Nov. 1771 wch reduced it to the State as appears in the
e View. The Violence of the flood, being the highest ever known, at first threw down 2 of the Arches.
ers were so shatter'd that 2 more fell a few days after. Together with these 4 Arches fell 23 houses &
rs wch stood upon them; & 6 of the Inhabitants perished in the ruins of the first wch fell.

PH BEILBY, with whom THOMAS BEWICK served his apprenticeship.

III

63 The Thomas Brown flask
In flint glass.
Height 9 in.
Decor: Scroll with name
Thos Brown Nenthead and
dated 1769, in white
enamel. On reverse side a
pastoral shooting scene in
white enamel.
Ashmolean Museum,
Oxford, England

Photograph
Michael Dudley

112

64 The Clavering Goblet
Large ogee bowl with opaque twist stem. Normal foot.
Height $7\frac{5}{8}$ in.
Decor: Inscribed words *Liberty & Clavering For Ever* in white, within a scroll in yellow enamel. Reverse floral garland and fruiting vine in white

enamel. Probably by Mary Beilby.
Victoria and Albert Museum, London
Photograph
Photo-Mayo

65 Heavy bottom flange tumbler designed as a firing glass.
Height 3 in.
Decor: A Masonic emblem in brilliant yellow enamel by William Beilby, with a floral garland in white enamel by Mary Beilby.
The Corning Museum of Glass, New York

Photograph
Alfred J. Wyatt

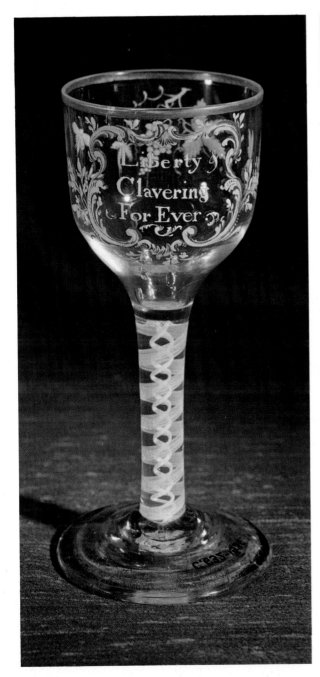

113

The Great Tyne Flood

In 1771, the Beilby family were to undergo a terrifying ordeal. For nearly a week there had been incessant heavy rains in the counties of Northumberland and Durham and on Sunday morning, 17 November, the River Tyne became a swirling, rising maelstrom and at about two o'clock in the morning it overflowed its banks at many points. A number of people were drowned in the upper reaches, but it was in Newcastle that the full ferocity of the river was felt.

With the bells of the churches sounding the alarm, the inhabitants woke to a terrifying night of horror. From the Skinnerburn to the Ouseburn, all the streets, including the Close, were underwater and a number of people were drowned in the cellars and basements before they could be warned. The glassmakers of Closegate and the Close suffered terribly and there was a panic to prevent the water reaching the furnaces. Some of them were completely inundated and rendered out of action for many months to come.

William and Ralph Beilby, with their sister Mary and their mother were, fortunately, safe on the higher ground of Forth Banks, but the two brothers left their point of safety to help as best they could in the work of salvage. Thomas Bewick, an athletic and strong figure, was an immense help and it is recorded that on several occasions he was seen wading up to his chest to help people to safety.

From a vantage point at the Castle Garth Stairs (see page 91, plate 49), the Beilby brothers were to witness the collapse of the Tyne Bridge, which had stood the brunt of five hundred years. A great emergency arose because the Magazine Tower (plate 66) at the end of the bridge was threatened. This gate served as a prison and the glassmakers of the Close rallied to help, moving the prisoners to the safety of the Closegate, in which they were housed on the second and third floors (see plate 16).

Six people were swept to their deaths with the destruction of the bridge and when dawn broke it was to reveal a terrifying scene. Three full-rigged schooners were high and dry on the streets; the river was still running high and carrying hundreds of dead animals down to the sea. Debris was piled up everywhere and all the glass houses, being so close to the river, had suffered terribly. The glassmakers, however, were amongst the first to recover, and only three days after the disaster, some of them were producing glass again.

After a week, the Tyne was running calm and serene again, and William Beilby completed a drawing of the ruins of the bridge. This was engraved by his brother Ralph and a reproduction of this actual engraving is shown in plate 62. It is interesting to observe the Latin used by William Beilby. *Delineat* (drawn by) William Beilby, and *Sculpsit* (engraved by) Ralph Beilby.

114

The Thomas Brown Flask

In 1769 William Beilby decorated a flask for Thomas Brown of the village of Nenthead in Cumberland (see plate 63). This village was an important lead-producing centre, and it is assumed that this commission was connected with the Cookson family, who had very important lead interests. The curious thing here is that although the front was clearly done by William, there appears another pastoral shooting scene on the side of the flask, which very much looks like the work of Mary. This can be seen if page 112 is turned on to one side. Notice particularly the 'Bewick' influence in the almost vignette type of pastoral figure and scene.

The Clavering Goblet

William Beilby carried out many commissions for masonic and political organizations. One of these is the large ogee goblet (page 113, plate 64) executed for Sir John Clavering (who was a bitter opponent of Warren Hastings) for his electioneering campaign. This goblet, with the inscription *Liberty & Clavering For Ever*, was probably completed by Mary Beilby. The floral and vine motif on the reverse side is typical of what is considered by the author to be the style and brushwork of Mary.

66 The Magazine Tower

115

67 Decanter and two wine glasses (matched)
Sloping shoulder fragmentary decanter in flint glass with ground and cut stopper. Height 12 in. (including stopper) Decor: Unidentified Arms

and scroll in full colour enamel. On reverse side fruiting vine in white enamel. On neck a scroll with Beilby butterfly. *Wine glasses*. Round funnel bowl with opaque twist stem. Normal foot.

Height 6 in. Decor: Fruiting vine in white enamel with double headed bird in brown and blue enamel. Traces of worn gilt rim.

Laing Art Gallery, Newcastle upon Tyne, England *Photograph* Photo-Mayo

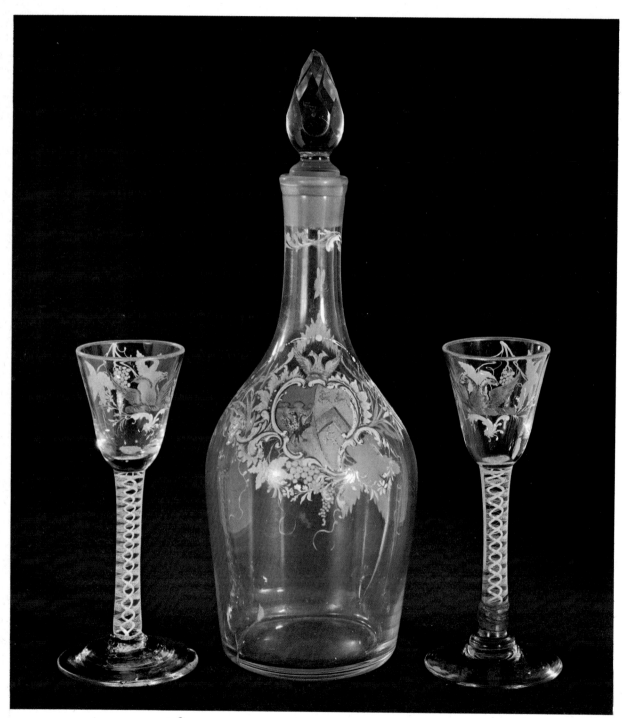

116

68 Two goblets

a) Bucket bowl with opaque twist stem and normal foot.
Height $7\frac{1}{2}$ in.
Decor: Superb example of entwined fruiting vine in white enamel.

b) Bucket bowl with opaque twist stem and normal foot.
Height $6\frac{1}{8}$ in.
Decor: Fruiting vine garland in white enamel.
Circa 1770.
The Lymbery Collection

Photograph
Photo-Mayo

117

The Corning Firing Glass
This is a short, flange-shaped tumbler with an extremely thick heavy bottom. The thick heavy base was used to tap on the table by the drinker, usually to show approval of the speaker or of a particular toast. This rare specimen (plate 65, page 113) was carried out for a Masonic Lodge. The Masonic emblem in brilliant yellow enamel was undoubtedly painted by William Beilby but the floral garland is very typical of the work of Mary Beilby.

The Laing Art Gallery
In about 1772 William Beilby executed a very fine decanter and set of opaque stem wine glasses on behalf of an unknown client. Only two glasses have survived the years and they are seen, with the decanter, on page 116, in plate 67. The decor was that of an unusual and unidentified Arms in colour with a typical Beilby vine motif. The double-headed eagle on the Arms suggests a continental origin but so far all efforts to identify them have failed.

This attractive set is the only exhibit of William Beilby, or the Beilby family, in their adopted city of Newcastle upon Tyne, and is on show at the Laing Art Gallery. It is extremely sad that the Laing Art Gallery's collection of Beilby pieces is so small when other museums in England have such excellent exhibits. There must be immense disappointment on the part of many connoisseurs of glass and fine art to find that the home of the Beilbys is so poorly served.

William and Mary
With the quick recovery of the Newcastle glass industry from the disaster of the great flood of 1771, William Beilby and his sister continued happily enough with their great work, but in 1772 William was much perturbed to find that the health of Mary was not good. He had observed the growing romance that had developed between young Thomas Bewick and his sister, but had not interfered when Ralph, the strict disciplinarian, had thrown cold water on the affair.

From 1772 onwards, Mary Beilby appears to have become something of an invalid and to have contributed very little to the work on glass, and early in 1774 came the cruellest of blows. Mary suffered a paralytic stroke, which disfigured and crippled her for the rest of her life. William felt the impact of this ultimate set-back much more so than the rest of the family. The sensitive and artistic Mary retired into a shell from which she never again fully emerged. William sustained her and stood by her in the sad years that followed. There is little doubt that his intense devotion to his sister materially affected his artistic output, and gradually the great work of the Beilby family came to an end.

118

In these later years many more noble families were to commission William Beilby, including The Earl of Rockingham (plate 54) and Thomas Vaughan of Dorset, who was associated with the designing and opening of the new Plymouth Dock for the Royal Navy in 1772 (pages 120 and 121, plates 69 and 70). The output for one man was quite phenomenal and the quality of the work to some extent varied. Certain works have obviously been produced to a price and are carried out on moderate quality glasses, such as the 'Success to the Swordmakers' tumbler, while at the other end of the scale, beautiful goblets like 'The Standard of Hesleyside' were specially designed, mouth-blown and hand finished, William Beilby completing the decor with his superb artistry.

The End
The end of the practical work of William Beilby, and indeed of the Beilby family as a whole, is extremely hard to establish. We find that no authentic and *dated* glasses appear after the Thomas Brown flask of 1769, but we do know that work definitely continued in Newcastle until 1778.

In 1776, according to the historian Hutchinson, 'There are upon the river two flint glaſs manufacturers'. These, of course, were Williams and Company and Airey, Cookson and Company. It was this year that the great Light Baluster Period of Newcastle Glass was to reach its peak, with these two firms the main participants.

In 1777 Thomas Bewick became the partner of Ralph Beilby after the termination of his apprenticeship, and the firm became known as 'Beilby and Bewick', with their workshop still at Amen Corner. Thomas Bewick has recorded that Ralph Beilby had virtually ceased his interest in glass from this time. William Beilby was then, for all practical purposes, alone in his work and still struggled with the finances of the household, for he appears in the Newcastle Directory of 1778 as running a drawing school in Northumberland Street, Newcastle.

The Family Break up
The break up of the Beilby family was to begin in the July of 1778 with the death of their cultured and courageous mother. This sad event is recorded in the *Newcastle Courant* of 4 July 1778: 'Sunday, Mrs. Beilby, mother of the ingenious Beilbys of this town.'

Even after the shock of his mother's death, William still struggled on. On 3 October 1778, he inserted an advertisement in the *Newcastle Journal* thanking his patrons and informing them that he proposed to hold an exhibition of the drawings and paintings of his pupils in Northumberland Street, Newcastle. This is the last tangible

119

69 and 70 The Thomas Vaughan Goblet
Bucket bowl with opaque twist stem. Normal foot. Height 7 in.
Decor: Crest and Arms of Thomas Vaughan of Dorset, Gloucestershire and Wiltshire in full colour enamel with the inscription *Thos Vaughan* and *Plymouth Dock* in white enamel on the reverse. *Circa* 1772.
Cecil Higgins Art Gallery, Bedford

Photograph
Photo-Mayo

120

and written association we can find in any records of William Beilby with his beloved city of Newcastle upon Tyne. After that date what we know of William Beilby and his sister Mary is pure mystery and conjecture, with a tiny piece of evidence here and there to give us a little, if very tantalizing, light. One thing is fairly certain, and that is that there appears to have been no further glass decorated by William Beilby.

For many decades now it has been assumed that William and Mary Beilby retired to Fifeshire in Scotland, where Mary died, but more recent researches by the author have thrown a little more light on this period, making conversely, conjectures on this period even more nebulous.

After 1778 William Beilby did not *immediately* go to Scotland with Mary; this was to happen some years later. Thomas Bewick gives us a clue when writing about Mary after her paralytic stroke in his *Memoir*: 'Long after this, she went with her eldest brother into Fifeshire where she died.' What is meant in this context by 'long after'? What happened was that William realized that after the partnership with Thomas Bewick, he had no future with his brother Ralph, especially when learning from Ralph that he was likely to be married soon. So William did not go to Fifeshire – he went to London sometime during 1779 and established a school which became known as The Battersea Academy.

Battersea

So much time has been spent on research in Battersea with so little result it would appear that, like so many famous people before him, William was swallowed up by the enormous metropolitan 'maw' of London and something of his genius and greatness was lost.

We now know for certain that he reached London in 1779 and very quickly became a pillar of the church in Battersea, for it is recorded that he became 'President of the Vestry' and that he ran a private school in the village.

There is one positive record that the author has not as yet been able to trace, and that is that there was a print published of 'Mr Beilby's Academy' where young gentlemen were boarded and taught Latin and Greek. The print was engraved by a Mr Skelton and drawn by William Beilby. All this fits in with what we know of William Beilby in Newcastle with his deep religious beliefs and his eagerness to help people. Battersea records show that William Beilby appeared first as a gentleman leaseholder in 1781 and that he was referred to as a schoolmaster until 1788.

It is very nice to record one pleasant link between William Beilby and his brother Ralph, who was still in Newcastle. The historian,

122

Thomas Brand, was a close friend of Ralph's, and for a period worked as secretary to the Duke of Northumberland in Northumberland House, London. He exchanged a great number of interesting letters with Ralph Beilby, so interesting that afterwards they were published in book form. In one of these letters, dated 23 June 1787, he records that he had called and passed on good wishes to his brother William at Battersea where he was 'Master of Battersea Academy'.

One vital point which cannot be cleared up is whether Mary was with William at Battersea during this period. There is no mention of Mary at any time, nor is there any indication that she assisted William or carried out any work of any kind. It can only be presumed that Mary was with William Beilby the whole of this time for it cannot be imagined that William would have abandoned her. From all that is known of William he was a thoughtful and kindly man and he would undoubtedly have attended his distressed sister with great care and devotion.

Marriage

At the age of forty-five, surprisingly late, William Beilby was to marry. The announcement was as follows: '12th November 1785. William Beilby Jnr., Master of Battersea Academy, second son of William Beilby Snr., to Ellen Purton of Putney.'

When one expresses the point 'surprisingly late', it is perhaps not so surprising when one considers the long years of care William had devoted to his sister Mary and to the rest of his family.

Very little is known of Ellen Purton, excepting that she was about twenty-five years younger than William and that she was the niece of a very wealthy City businessman, a Mr Falconer. There is no doubt that Mr Falconer must have been immensely impressed with William Beilby because it is recorded that he purchased a large agricultural estate in Fifeshire and retired there, taking with him his niece Ellen and William Beilby, as either secretary or manager. It is here where the mystery returns, for no trace can be found in Fifeshire of any such estate, in spite of the most exhaustive searches. There is little doubt however, that it was in about 1788 (the end of his recorded lease in Battersea) that William Beilby left London together with his wife and his sister and took up residence in Scotland.

On 28 August 1788, John Brand writes again to Ralph Beilby from Alnwick Castle, Northumberland:

'I need not add I should have been very glad also to have seen your brother William, whom, by the by, I hardly dare look in the face. When the yoke of 'Newcastle' is taken from my shoulder, I hope I shall make amends for my seeming neglect to him and all my friends.'

The 'yoke' John Brand refers to means the *History of Newcastle*, which he was at that time writing and which has become one of the great literary legacies of Newcastle's past. But John Brand makes no further reference to William or his possible move to Fifeshire so we are left again with conjecture.

Before leaving the subject of the John Brand letters, it is perhaps a great pity that they are all 'one sided', for we have only Brand's letters and none of Ralph Beilby's replies.

Fifeshire

This period of the saga of William Beilby is undoubtedly for a researcher, the most frustrating. From all the evidence, we are certain that William moved to Fifeshire with his wife and with the pathetic Mary. According to MacKenzie, another well-known Newcastle historian: 'Having married the niece of Mr. Falconer, a rich manufacturer in London, who afterwards purchased a large estate in Fifeshire, Scotland, he removed to that place, where he displayed the versatility of his genius by conducting the agricultural improvements upon his uncle's property.'

So many questions remain unanswered. Where was this estate in Fifeshire? If Mary Beilby died in Fifeshire, when did she die and where is she buried? When did William Beilby and his wife leave Fifeshire and why? After intensive research through dozens of parish registers, estate records, even with the assistance of every archivist and senior librarian in Fifeshire and the Lowlands, all these questions remain unanswered, and we are left again with conjecture.

After apparently living on this estate in Fifeshire it appears that at last Mary died in 1797. Not long afterward the wealthy uncle died, followed soon by his wife and thus unexpectedly, Mrs William Beilby found herself the heir to a considerable fortune. What happened then is incomprehensible, for one would have thought that being comfortably off they would have enjoyed the advantages of living in comfort on a country estate. Possibly the death of Mary had an unsettling affect on William and it is possible that there were restricting codicils in the bequest to his wife. Whatever the reasons, William Beilby and his wife left Fifeshire and took up residence in Hull. The choice of Hull is a curious one and it can only be presumed that Mrs Beilby had some connections there through her relations.

Before leaving the question of Fifeshire one must consider the question of whether any work on glass was carried out by William Beilby during his stay there. It has been the subject of contemplation whether certain enamel Jacobite glasses with the head of Prince Charles Edward Stuart were carried out by William Beilby. The author has examined these very closely and they cannot be con-

125

sidered to be by William Beilby by any stretch of the imagination. First of all, the glasses are definitely not Newcastle and the enamel work is clumsy with none of the delicacy of touch of William Beilby, although they are interesting as specimens of other glass enamel work.

In Scotland there are very few specimens of Beilby glass. Only one piece is in the Royal Scottish Museum and the others can be traced to Newcastle sources, so that in the absence of new and extraordinary evidence, it must be concluded, somewhat regretfully, that no work on glass was executed by William Beilby while he was living in Scotland.

There remains in this context one final point which must throw a spanner in the works of accepted theory concerning the Beilbys in Fifeshire. The author has recently found a most interesting and previously unpublished letter in the archives of The Literary and Philosophical Society of Newcastle upon Tyne from the widow of Ralph Beilby to the Reverend A. Hedley dated 28 December 1822 (see page 87).

Disregarding all other aspects of this letter, the vital reference is to William Beilby having married 'a lady of large fortune twenty-five years younger than himself and resided with her in *Perthshire* more than twenty years' – Perthshire – *not* Fifeshire. Was Mrs Ralph Beilby right and have we all been searching in the wrong area of Scotland? Or was Mrs Beilby, at this late stage of her life, rather confused? Apart from the reference to Perthshire, the time of twenty years does not seem to tally. The author has extended the search to cover Perthshire, but so far with the same completely negative results. So, for the time being, we must leave it there and turn our attention to the final phase of William Beilby; his life and death in Hull.

Hull
After an immense amount of research, the date William Beilby and his wife arrived in Hull still cannot be established. The first positive record we can find is in the Hull Directory of 1814 (in which the spelling was wrong): '1814 Bielby William, Drawing Master, 6 South Street' and this continued until 1817 when the spelling was corrected to Beilby. In 1817, the following entry appears: '1817 Beilby William, Gent, English St.' It would appear that William Beilby lived with his wife for quite a number of years in English Street, but no record can be found that any work on glass was carried out. It may be a coincidence, but English Street was very close to a glass house on the side of the River Humber at Humber Bank, but no link can be established between William Beilby and this glass house.

126

The question which must be placed against the Beilbys' stay in Hull is the fact that they lived in English Street, which could not be considered to be by any means a fashionable residential area. It is curious that Mrs William Beilby, who had inherited a 'fortune' came to live in such a modest, if respectable, area. There are no records, or even circumstantial evidence, to assist us in assessing this period.

There were two sons and one daughter of William Beilby's marriage, but the directories of Hull for the period only record one son, William Turton Beilby, as a clerk, and living at the same address in English Street in 1822.

It appears that William Beilby devoted most of this late period of his life to the Church and to works of charity. It is sad that this great artist was to decorate no more glass, and all we find is a number of modestly executed water colours, certain of which are still in private hands today in the Hull area.

The final curtain was to fall on the life of William Beilby when he died at 4 English Street, Hull on Friday, 8 October 1819. We must presume that he was buried in the old cemetery of the Church of the Holy Trinity, which was fairly close to English Street, but no trace can be found of any memorial or tombstone.

His obituary appeared in the Hull local newspaper and a brief notice was to appear in the *Newcastle Courant*. The Hull tribute was as follows:

'Yesterday, aged 81, William Beilby, of this town, gent. A man in whom were all the social and amiable qualities united, and perhaps a brighter example of unaffected Christian goodness, with a steady faith in Christ, never left this transitory world; in the immediate circle of his friends he shone conspicuously for every thing that could make social and communicative bliss enchanting; his death like his life involuntary demands – "May my last end be like his".'

Perhaps an effusive tribute, but among the many mourners on that day so long ago, could any of them have realized the true glory, in art, of William Beilby, 'gent'?

128

14 A Beilby masterpiece

72 and 73 Bowl
Chelsea-shape bowl in blown crystal glass.
Width $9\frac{7}{8}$ in.
Decor: Unidentified Arms and trophy forms in white and colour enamels.
Elaborate rococo scroll with lace pattern to rim. Gilt rim.
Dated 1765.
Victoria and Albert Museum, London
Photograph
Photo-Mayo

Of all the great works attributed to William Beilby, the English Glass Bowl (plates 72 and 73) is considered by many connoisseurs of glass as his finest achievement. This bowl is at present in the Glass and Ceramic Section of the Victoria and Albert Museum in London and should, if humanly possible, be seen in its actual form.

The bowl is a pure – what we in England would call 'Chelsea' shape – and of full finely blown crystal and without any defects. William Beilby put all his skills to use here. There are two unidentified Coats of Arms in delicate colours, while on opposing sides are two panels indicating some form of naval or national trophy. Linking up the Arms and panels is the most exquisite rococo scroll work and filling in to the rim is a delicate lace pattern. The resulting effect is to make this bowl one of the most pleasant and attractive of all William Beilby's work. The technical achievement of firing the enamels into this finely blown crystal bowl without distortion was remarkable.

Finally, for our record, it was signed *Beilby Invt & pinxt* and dated *Newcastle 1765*. The fact that the initial was not on this signature should not for one moment disturb the reader. A comparison of this signature with that of *W. Beilby* on the Fitzwilliam Museum Royal Goblet shown in plate 2 leaves no doubts as to its provenance.

Many authors have made the mistake of presuming that there is *no* initial to the signature of the Fitzwilliam Goblet. A closer examination will reveal that the 'W' is monogrammed into the 'B' of Beilby; the superb glass bowl in the Victoria and Albert Museum is definitely by William Beilby.

15 The Margaret and Winneford Bowl

Since the writing of the preceding chapter 'A Beilby Masterpiece', there has been a most important 'discovery' of a companion bowl to the one described. This second bowl most elegantly decorated by William Beilby, was privately commissioned to commemorate the launching on the Tyne of the good ship *The Margaret and Winneford* on behalf of the Forster family of Bamburgh, Northumberland. The launching is almost certain to have been in 1765, as both bowls were undoubtedly made and decorated at the same time, and the specimen in the Victoria and Albert Museum is dated 1765.

130

74 Armorial ship bowl
Front
English Chelsea shape in flint glass.
Diameter $9\frac{1}{2}$ in., height $4\frac{1}{2}$ in.
Decor: By William Beilby. The English ship *The Margaret and Winneford* with full sail in colour enamel. The main body of the bowl is decorated with a rich lace pattern in white enamel. The interior of the bowl has a most elegant white swan with elevated wings, and this rare feature is clearly seen in plate 75. This rare and beautiful bowl is reproduced in full colour here for the first time. It is similar to the masterpiece by William Beilby in the Victoria and Albert Museum, London. Auctioned at Sotheby's on 23 November 1970, and purchased by the author.
The Laing Art Gallery, Newcastle upon Tyne
Photograph
Photo-Mayo

75
The inside base of the Margaret and Winneford bowl showing the white rising swan and covering the pontil mark of the bowl. This is the only known Beilby specimen with this unusual and charming feature.

76 *Reverse*
The rim is gilt with the arms of the Forster family of Bamburgh, Northumberland, supported by a feathery rococo scroll in white enamel.

131

16 The Standard of Hesleyside

One of the most romantic commissions entrusted to William Beilby was the designing, making and decorating of the famous glass known as 'The Standard of Hesleyside'.

So little is known of the life of William Beilby that even the smallest glimpse is rewarding, and fortunately, we have in the Standard not only a positive date of 1763, but also a wonderful romantic story to go with it.

The commissioning of the Standard of Hesleyside was effected by the Lord of the Manor of one of Northumberland's oldest and most noble families, the Charltons of Hesleyside. He was Edward Charlton, a great scion of a great family, whose ancestry goes back in England to before the Domesday Book. His striking portrait, which still hangs in the grand hall of Hesleyside, is reproduced in plate 77.

In the early part of 1763 Edward Charlton, with one of his cousins, paid one of their rare visits to Newcastle on horseback. Sauntering past the Cathedral and the crowded narrow walk known as Amen Corner, he noticed a most interesting shop alongside the churchyard, with the name 'Beilby and Company'. They were well-known engravers, and Edward remembered some work he wished to place. He was very impressed with the bearing of the owner of this business, who introduced himself as Ralph Beilby. Ralph was obviously a man of culture and education and Edward Charlton was even more impressed by some very fine and handsome glass goblets which lay half completed on a work bench. Ralph explained that this was the work of his elder brother William. William Beilby was then introduced and discussed in some detail the technical and artistic nature of his work. William was a much quieter person than his brother Ralph, who was obviously the business head of the family.

As a result of this meeting Edward Charlton placed a special commission with William Beilby to design a goblet which would take the capacity of a full bottle of claret (in those days there was no Government legislation on the size of bottles, and a bottle of claret would have held between twenty and twenty-four fluid ounces of

132

wine). This obviously would have to be a very tall and handsome goblet to take twenty-four fluid ounces. The goblet was specially designed and was probably made in one of the two flint glass houses at that time in production at the Closegate.

The decoration of the goblet was carried out by William Beilby in white and colour enamels and bears the inscription *The Standard of Hesleyside* in italic, roman and gothic lettering. There is a rococo scroll in yellow and red surrounding the inscription. On the reverse side, there is the Charlton Crest (lion rampant) enamelled in red, with the name *Edward Charlton Esq*^{r} in white. Vine-leaf and fruiting vine complete the decoration.

The goblet itself (illustrated in plates 78 and 79) is most interesting and, being specially designed and hand made, is unique. The glass is of brilliant white metal with a fairly stout opaque twist stem. The bowl is a conventional rounded funnel type but immediately beneath is the most unusual feature of a second bowl in bulbous form and connecting with the main bowl. This was obviously designed to make the task of 'sinking the Standard' more difficult.

Thus was this priceless Beilby heirloom and treasure fashioned and created. Edward Charlton, when he commissioned the Standard, could hardly have realized the tradition he had begun.

After the safe delivery of the Standard to Hesleyside, which is a beautiful and remote manor house in the North Tyne valley border area of Northumberland, it was established as a tradition of manhood that the full Standard of Claret be drained at a single draught. Many came to Hesleyside to drink the Standard, but most were unsuccessful.

Sinking the Standard

Down through the years has come a most interesting and amusing description of a successful double draining of the Standard. This description was given by the great lady of Hesleyside, Barbara Charlton, who was well known to Queen Victoria. She describes the event as follows:

'In August, back at Hesleyside, we gave a house-warming and entertained a great deal of company; Mr and Mrs Plowden, Marmion Ferrars, Mr Scrope and his two daughters Florence and Adela, Edward, afterwards Cardinal, Howard, Edward Riddell of The Grange, Kate Strickland, Fanny Blackett, Sir Joseph and Lady Ratcliffe and son and two daughters, Francis Cholmeley, and Mr and Mrs Murray. Mr Murray was at the Foreign Office, and was the man, much later on, who caused commotion by tearing up as so much waste paper, King Thibaw's offer of marriage to Queen Victoria. In the evening there was dancing, for with Adela Scrope and Edward

133

77 Edward Charlton
who commissioned 'The
Standard of Hesleyside'.
In a private home
Photograph
Photo-Mayo

134

78 Goblet
'The Standard of
Hesleyside'. Deep round
funnel bowl connecting
with bulbous lower bowl.
Short thick opaque twist
stem with bluish colouring.
Height 11 in.
Decor: *Front* Inscription
The Standard of Hesleyside
in white enamel

within a scroll of golden
yellow.

79 *Reverse*
The Charlton Arms in
colour, with the inscription
Edward Charlton Esqr 1763
and fruiting vine motif in
white enamel. Worn gilt
rim. Foot and stem broken
but repaired.
In a private collection
Photograph
Photo-Mayo

135

Howard of the party it simply had to be. The future cardinal was then about twenty, and, although he talked about diplomacy, had not fixed on a career. He was a splendid linguist. Eventually he went into the Guards, and after a few years abandoned soldiering for the Church. A treasured family possession was then, and still is, a very beautiful Newcastle glass goblet, probably of eighteenth-century workmanship and most richly ornamented 'The Standard of Hesleyside'. It held a bottle of claret, neither more nor less, and it was the custom and a challenge, originating in Jacobite days, to gulp the contents down without taking breath. On the occasion of our house-warming it was once brought out at supper, and the swallowing feat was duly performed by two daring youths, Edward Howard and a young clergyman, a Mr Gibbs. As far as could be seen, neither was the worse for it, as they both danced steadily after supper. I always dreaded this calling for the Standard, for some boasters immediately succumbed to the gluttonous operation before they could reach their rooms, and such an exhibition before ladies was not quite in keeping with the refinement of the times. Many times I suggested that the convivial vessel should be put under a glass case and kept in the drawing-room; but I was always voted down, and in due course it suffered damage by the handling of a drunken butler. . . .'

Incidentally, the advice of Barbara Charlton was ultimately carried out and after the Standard had been expertly repaired it was placed in a handsome glass and brass bound case, where it remains at Hesleyside, still with the Charlton family, to this day.

How delightful also to reflect that a future Cardinal of the Church of Rome should be such a man of the world.

The Spur in the Dish
There is another legend connected with the Standard of Hesleyside which is of great interest.

In the sixteenth century Hesleyside, near the Scottish border, was an area very vulnerable to the constant raids of the Scots into England, and as Lord of the Manor of Hesleyside, the male head of the family was entrusted by the King to lead the punitive and retaliatory raids to pay back the Scots. The men of the North Tyne area and the border needed no second invitation, and when they were summoned to assemble at Hesleyside, it was a convivial and colourful, although warlike, occasion.

The legend of The Spur in the Dish was enacted when the lady of Hesleyside, quite sick of the general drinking and carousing among the men, with no sign of their setting out on a retaliatory raid, ceremoniously arrived with food demanded by the master.

136

To the chagrin of the assembled company, when the silver cover was removed there was revealed a single spur instead of the anticipated roast beef – a calculated and very successful rebuff to tell them that the larder was empty and they had better 'set about their business'.

A painting of the enacted ceremony of The Spur in the Dish hangs in the Grand Hall at Wallington in Northumberland and is reproduced in plate 80. It is preserved by the National Trust and is part of a series depicting Northumbrian history throughout the ages.

The most interesting point about this legend and painting is that the Standard of Hesleyside appears in the painting, to the left hand side of the Master of Hesleyside, the central figure with the beard seated at the dining table.

Ride, Rowly, ride, now the hough's i' the pot!

The Spur in the Dish warns the Border-chief that the Larder needs replenishing

138

80 The Spur in the Dish
Wallington Hall,
Northumberland
Photograph
Philipson & Son Ltd.

81 Ale glass
Deep round funnel bowl
with opaque twist stem and
normal foot.
Height $6\frac{7}{8}$ in.
Decor: Beehive with bees
in flight supported by scroll
and passion flower in white
enamel. Worn gilt rim.
Decorated probably by
Mary Beilby.
Circa 1765.
The Lymbery Collection
Photograph
Photo-Mayo

139

17 Mary Beilby

Mary Beilby must be considered the most remote and mythical character in the fascinating Beilby saga. She was born in Durham City in February of 1750 and was baptized at St Nicholas' Church, Durham on 12 February. She was educated privately in the City of Durham and although there was another sister Elizabeth in the male-dominated family, she was the darling of her brothers and the real favourite of her parents.

From an early age she showed the same strong artistic talents that were so much a feature of the Beilby family. After the return of her brothers William and Richard from Birmingham in 1760, she was to learn from them the art of drawing and although she was only eleven she showed a surprising aptitude for painting.

When the family were struggling against financial difficulties, Mary was of great practical and moral support to her mother, especially after the early marriage of her sister Elizabeth. With the move of the family to Gateshead in 1760, Mary Beilby actively assisted her mother in the school they had established and she continued teaching for quite some years.

The establishment of the engraving business at Amen Corner by Ralph and William very much excited her and she became a familiar figure there. She adored her brother William, and as she grew older, hardly ever left his side. They romped around the old town of Newcastle together, continually exploring the medieval walls, the narrow chares and the teeming business centre. Of all their many adventures together Mary loved to visit the glassmakers at Closegate best of all.

At first they used to walk across the front of the old Castle and down the enthralling Castle Garth Stairs to the Close and on to Closegate, but after a while William showed her a much more exciting route. This was from Amen Corner across what is now called Hanover Square, toward Forth Banks, where stood the formidable Whitefriars Tower (see page 35, plate 18) on the very brink of the river bank. At this point the old city wall joined the tower and steeply descended to Closegate where all the glass houses were concentrated.

140

Alongside the Whitefriars Tower were the most terrifying stairs leading to Closegate, appropriately called the 'Breakneck Stairs'. Mary loved these stairs and when she reached the glass houses at Closegate she was entranced by the magic of glassmaking.

Mary, although very shy, was acutely aware of the importance of the experiments her brother William was making in the firing of the colour pigments into the transparent white crystal glass and must undoubtedly have assisted at times. The glassmakers, always very strict in convention, must have looked askance at the slight girl who always seemed to be with William Beilby, but they had a great sense of courtesy and in the end must have accepted her as one of them. The actual work she carried out on glass and which was fired in their own muffle furnaces must have earned their respect.

When she was fourteen William Beilby was already passing on to her certain work on simple glasses, and also instructing her in the art of mixing and grinding pigments for hand painting. Most of her early work was simple floral garlands (plates 50, 51(b) and 82) and then vine motifs and rococo scrolls (plates 63 and 84(b)). Later on, no doubt, after instruction from Ralph, she was to carry out inscribed work with the simpler type of commissions (plate 83). Although excellent in her own way, she never quite attained the perfection of her brother William.

Ill-fated Romance
The year 1767, when Mary Beilby was eighteen years of age, was to be for her probably the most emotional year in her life for it was then that the young Thomas Bewick, aged fourteen, was apprenticed to her brother Ralph. Poor Mary – she was never really to have a chance in the ill-fated romance which followed the arrival of Thomas. We can never really know what went on in the mind of Mary Beilby during this period, but one's heart must go out to her. We have the account, brief and graphic, from the pen of Thomas but, alas, nothing from Mary.

When Thomas arrived it was fairly obvious that the pair, by reason of their common work, would be together much of the time. Naturally, with the very strict upbringing of Mary, their association would be kept within extremely narrow bounds and we already know how Thomas, in the early days of his apprenticeship, was often in trouble. Nevertheless, the romance developed and must have been carefully nurtured by Mary. One must picture the many occasions when the couple must have worked together and of course at night in the family household they had meals and entertainment together. When the young Thomas was instructed to read to old Mrs Beilby, it is fairly certain that Mary would have been present.

141

82 Three wine glasses
(a) Round funnel bowl,
opaque twist stem. Normal
foot.
Height 6 in.
Decor: Floral garland in
white enamel.
Circa 1765.
(b) Deep round funnel bowl,
air twist stem. Normal foot.
Height $6\frac{1}{8}$ in.
Decor: Scroll garland in
white enamel.
Circa 1765.
(c) Ogee optic bowl. Opaque
twist stem. Normal foot.
Height $5\frac{3}{4}$ in.
Decor: Scroll and flower
garland in white enamel.
Circa 1765.
All three of these delightful
small glasses were almost
certainly decorated by
Mary Beilby.
Fitzwilliam Museum
Photograph
Photo-Mayo

83 Firing glass
Loaded conical funnel bowl,
with squat heavy air twist
stem. Heavy foot.
Height 4 in.
Decor: Inscribed word
Temperance within a scroll
in white enamel.
Circa 1765.
The Lymbery Collection
Photograph
Photo-Mayo

142

84 Three wine glasses
(a) Trumpet bowl, with
drawn air twist stem.
Normal foot.
Height $6\frac{3}{4}$ in.
Decor: Fruiting vine in
white enamel.
(b) Ogee bowl, with opaque
twist stem. Normal foot.
Height 6 in.
Decor: Fruiting vine in
white enamel.
(c) Trumpet bowl, with
fine mesh opaque twist
stem. Normal foot.
Height $6\frac{7}{8}$ in.
Circa 1770.
Fitzwilliam Museum
Photograph
Photo-Mayo

85 Two wine glasses
(a) Round funnel bowl with
opaque twist stem. Normal
foot.
Height 6 in.
Decor: Pyramid with
pastoral scene in white
enamel. Thin gilt rim.
(b) Round funnel bowl with
opaque twist stem. Normal
foot.
Height $5\frac{7}{8}$ in.
Decor: Classical ruins and
pastoral setting in white
enamel. Thin gilt rim.
Circa 1765.
Both of these glasses are
considered to be executed
by Mary Beilby in the early
wash enamel period. The
brushwork is quite coarse
and contrasts sharply with
the finer work on the vine
motifs of the three glasses
above.
The Lymbery Collection
Photograph
Photo-Mayo

143

We have the evidence of Thomas Bewick's *Memoir* that 'I had formed a strong attachment to her, but I could not make this known to her or to anyone else'; but nothing from Mary. The heart of Mary must have leapt with joy when she saw how Thomas was making a dramatic success, and perhaps never more so than when he attained the award of The Society of Arts in London.

The poignant end to this love story is difficult to write and even more so to assess, but it can perhaps be best presented in the actual words of the second most important person involved – Thomas Bewick, in that extract from his *Memoir*. The choice of 'second' is deliberate, for surely we must in all conscience accord the prime place to the hapless, forlorn and forsaken Mary Beilby.

'From the length of time I had known and noticed Miss Beilby, I had formed a strong attachment to her, but I could not make this known to her or to anyone else. I could have married her before I was done with my apprenticeship without any fears on my part, but I felt for her, and pined and fretted at so many bars being in the way of our union. One of the greatest was the supposed contempt in which I was held by the rest of the family, who, I thought, treated me with great hauteur, though I had done everything in my power to oblige them. I had, like a stable boy, waited upon their horse; and had cheerfully done everything they wanted at my hands till one of the brothers grossly affronted me in the business of the stable. This I instantly resented, and refused attendance there any more. Before I was out of my time, Miss Beilby had a paralytic stroke, which very greatly altered her look, and rendered her for some time unhappy. Long after this she went with her eldest brother into Fifeshire, where she died.'

Nothing more can be written about Mary Beilby; her sufferings must have been great. They are covered in the limited extent that research has allowed in the chapter devoted to her brother William.

If consolation can be written into this sad story it must be that Mary Beilby was sustained ultimately by the devotion of her brother in Newcastle, London and Scotland. Whether she died in Fifeshire or Perthshire we shall probably never know, nor where Mary Beilby was laid to rest but she will be remembered as few women of the arts will be remembered.

We have no picture or etching to remember her by; we have no writings and no signatures on any of her works; we do not, for certainty, know any of the paintings she actually executed.

Yet she *will* be remembered. In hundreds of years and decades from now historians and writers on art will look at the great works on glass attributed to William and Mary Beilby and will say 'I wonder what "she" was really like.'

144

18 Thomas Bewick

'O now that the genius of Bewick were mine, and the skill he learnt on the banks of the Tyne.'

WORDSWORTH

It is not the object of this work to write a life-story of Thomas Bewick, which has been done many times before, and best of all perhaps by Thomas Bewick himself in his remarkable *Memoir*. All that is intended is to cover the important aspects where, like a tapestry, they interweave with the colourful threads of the Beilby story.

Thomas Bewick was essentially a man of the earth – all his life he was never far removed from the soil of his beloved Northumbrian countryside. In the words of his father 'an unruly boy', he rebelled against petty discipline and tyranny from any source, were it a schoolmaster, parent, workmates or master.

His love of drawing got him into many scrapes; 'I spent as much time as I could in filling with my pencil all the unoccupied spaces with representations of such objects as struck my fancy. As soon as I filled all the blank spaces in my books, I had recourse, at all spare times, to the gravestones, and the floor of the church porch with a bit of chalk.' During this period of Thomas Bewick's childhood and early youth he lived very close to nature and this was reflected strongly in all his drawings. The chase of the fox, the baiting of otters, badgers and foumarts, poaching of various kinds, fishing, following the hunt, were all part of his background. The shock he suffered at some of these 'sports' made him very sensitive throughout his life to the sufferings of animals and his great love of living creatures is strongly reflected in his great works.

As a boy he did practically everything from milking the cows, 'mucking out' the byre, watching the lambs throughout the night on the bleak moors, watching the birds driven to shelter from the severity of the storms, swimming in the Tyne stark naked, holding communion with 'my intimate acquaintances' the robins, wrens, blackbirds, sparrows and the rarer game birds such as woodcock, snipe, redwing and pheasant.

Thomas Bewick loved to listen to the talk of the menfolk of the

145

86 Newcastle Scene
(Bewick woodcut)
Perhaps a boyhood memory
of Thomas Bewick playing
with his friends. In the
background, to the left,
the Cathedral spire of
St Nicholas, Newcastle upon
Tyne, while on the right, a
colliery on the south bank of
the Tyne.

district. They were mostly rough-hewn Northumbrian stock, poor cottagers and the like, but they had an independence of spirit which was astonishing. He was to learn from them the language of the stars and planets, local history, border ballads of wild and poetic quality. Thomas Bewick was impressed with the tough kindly humour of the pitmen who worked for his father, and the old soldiers, of whom he wrote 'they were magnificent'. The stories, simply told, of the battles fought by these old soldiers left an indelible impression on his mind.

One of them, John Cowie, described the battle of Minden in minute detail and how 'in the absence of Lord Sackville, they shook hands the whole length of the line, vowing to stand by each other without flinching'. John Cowie had served with Napier's Grenadiers and occasionally, as the spirit moved him, he appeared in his old military coat. Thomas Bewick was obviously moved when this old soldier died and probably even more so when afterwards he was to see Cowie's military coat, which had been shot at at Minden, hanging up on a stake in the corn field as a scarecrow. This must have remained on his mind for many years, for he was to execute a woodcut vignette which appeared in Volume I of his classic *The History of Birds* (plate 88), an example of Bewick's ironic humour – the scarecrow that does not even scare crows, a final indignity.

The Apprentice
At length came the momentous meeting with Ralph and William Beilby, which led to the apprenticeship of Thomas Bewick to Ralph on 1 October 1767, and which has been described in the Ralph Beilby chapter.

From the beginning, Thomas Bewick's independence of spirit was to lead him into trouble during his apprenticeship; and he became

146

a well known, if boisterous, spirit amongst the very busy tradesmen around the red brick workshop at Amen Corner. Many of the shops along Denton Chare were occupied by fruiterers and confectioners and the young Thomas was often seen hatless and always dashing towards his lodging at the Forth; and they would remark 'there goes Beilby's wild lad'.

The romance between Thomas Bewick and Ralph Beilby's sister Mary has already been described, and nothing much more can be added to it, except that it must have had a profound effect on his mind and considerably altered the trend of his work. The break, when it did come, must have been very complete and absolute for Thomas Bewick never mentioned Mary Beilby again in his *Memoir* and in due course was to marry Isabella Elliot of Ovingham, a childhood friend well known to his family.

On the termination of Thomas Bewick's apprenticeship on 1 October 1774, he found himself at liberty to enjoy some degree of travel and visited Carlisle, Scotland and the Border Country on foot.

On 1 October 1776, after a somewhat harrowing sea coast passage in a collier from Newcastle, he arrived in London, where he was surprised to find that his reputation had preceded him and he was to find many good friends and associates.

Although he had planned to stay in London and build a business there, it was not long before the call of his native Northumberland drew him back. The vastness of London appalled him, and although much of the cultural life appealed to him, he had to say frankly 'I did not like London; it appeared to me a world of itself where everthing in the extreme might at once be seen: extreme riches, extreme poverty, extreme grandeur, and extreme wretchedness – all of which I had not contemplated before. For my part, I am still of the same mind that I was when I left London, and that is that I would rather be herding sheep on Mickley Bank Top than remain in London, although for doing so I might become premier of England.'

On returning to Newcastle, Thomas Bewick became a partner to his old master Ralph Beilby under the name of 'Beilby and Bewick' at Amen Corner. This partnership, although successful from a business standpoint, was in many ways unhappy for both of them. In both of their major works of collaboration, *The History of Quadrupeds* and *The History of Birds*, they disputed bitterly and somewhat sadly, this is described in the Ralph Beilby chapter.

An assessment of the works of Thomas Bewick is almost beyond modern comprehension. Ruskin wrote of him 'I know of no drawing so subtle as Bewick's since the fifteenth century, excepting Holbein's and Turner's'. His great fame came at a time when the art of woodcuts for printing in England had reached a very low ebb. Thomas

147

87 Fishing (Bewick woodcut)
Another boyhood memory.
Fishing in one of the many
Northumberland rivers.
There appears to be a moral
about this vignette. The
roughneck boy below is
apparently more successful
than the well dressed and
expensively equipped boy
sitting above.

88 Minden Scarecrow
(Bewick woodcut).

148

Bewick not only restored it, he gave it a new dimension; he brought into these beautifully executed woodcuts such infinite detail and absolute charm that even after detailed study, one can find in them new angles and new beauty.

In all his nature woodcuts of animals, birds and fish he brings an authentic quality which at once reveals the artist as a man who really lived with nature and who became part of it. The woodcuts are mostly very small about $3\frac{1}{2}$ in. $\times$ $2\frac{1}{2}$ in. and to achieve such detail is truly astonishing, especially the manner in which he portrays the changing weather, the seasons and the magnificent composition of the Northumbrian settings, and also the wonderful humour he brings into his characterizations of people (see plates 89, 90, 92, and 93).

As Thomas Bewick matured, the wildness of his youth had gone, but his immense independence of spirit remained with him; he became a philosopher of searching and sometimes searing truth. He loved Northumberland and he loved England; he was a true countryman.

The American War of Independence
During a great part of Thomas Bewick's life the American War of Independence was fought, and he saw, as very few people at that time saw, the immense long-term effects of that struggle. What he wrote as an Englishman at that time was devastatingly accurate and is fully reproduced here. It is very important for the reader to realize that at the time this was written the war had *just* ended and Cornwallis had surrendered at Yorktown.
'In reverting back to another look at the American War, one may reckon to a certainty of its having been made the subject of debatings, and of furnishing matter for the thinking part of mankind, over the whole of the civilized world. George the Third and his advizers did not, perhaps, think of this, nor its consequences; neither did they ever contemplate the mighty events they were thus bringing about in rearing and establishing the wisest and greatest republic and nation the world ever saw. When its immense territory is filled with an enlightened population, and its government, like a rock, founded on the liberties and the rights of man, it is beyond human comprehension to foresee the strides the nation will make towards perfection. It is likely they will cast a compassionate eye on the rest of the world, grovelling under arbitrary power, banish it from the face of the earth, and kill despots with a frown. One would fain hope, however, that kings and their advisers will coolly reflect upon the improving intellect of mankind, and will take measures to govern in a way more befitting the state of the people over whom they are called upon to rule.'

149

89 The Tombstones
(Bewick woodcut).

90 The Storm
(Bewick woodcut).

91 Northumbrian Scene
(Bewick woodcut).

150

92 Snow Scene
(Bewick woodcut).

93 Man at a Wall
(Bewick woodcut).

94 The End
(Bewick woodcut).

151

95 The Glassblowers of Closegate
(Bewick woodcut).
The only authentic impression we have of a Newcastle glass house. Thomas Bewick executed this woodcut about 1780. It can be clearly seen that it was a flint glass house from the goblet on the right, and so it must have been either Airey, Cookson and Company or John Williams and Company of Closegate.
See chapter 19

Patriotism and England

Also reproduced without apology is what Thomas Bewick wrote about Patriotism and England.

'Patriotism ought to direct every man to do honour to himself and to his country; and it is in this that great national power principally consists. It is also by the good conduct, and consequent character, of the great mass of the people that a nation is exalted. The crown – the richest diamond of our life – is the love of our country; and the man who neglects this, and ceases to reverence and adore his Maker, is good for nothing. The country, surrounded by the briny deep, where all our ancestors lie buried – in which from youth upwards we have felt the benefit of equal laws, first acted upon and handed down to us by the Great Alfred, and maintained from time to time amidst all the attempts of despotism to overturn them, – by men famed for matchless wisdom and virtue, – a country so renowned as England, so famous for all that most strongly attracts the admiration of men, – a country whose genius and power have, for ages, been such as to make her views and intentions an object of solicitude with every nation, and with every enlightened individual in the world, – a country famed for her laws, famed in arts and arms, famed for the struggles which, age after age, her sons have held with tyranny in every form it has assumed, – and, beyond all these, famed for having given birth to, and reared to manhood, those men of matchless

152

wisdom and virtue whose memories will be held up to admiration, and whose example will be followed in ages to come – who have rendered the very name of Englishmen respected in every civilized country in the world.'

The partnership with Ralph Beilby ended by mutual consent on 6 January 1798, and the business was carried on by Thomas Bewick, still in the old workshop at Amen Corner.

As the eighteenth century drew to its close, Thomas Bewick enrolled many pupils who were to continue the Bewick tradition and to establish themselves in their own right.

In his old age he became still further the philosopher and his writings on religion and the rights of man have become the subject of much controversy in the light of the modern permissive society. His final soliloquy is typical and it appears in the last page of his *Memoir*.

'In offering these my sentiments and opinions I have made in my passage through life, I have never intended to give offence to good men. With these sentiments some may be pleased and others displeased, but conscious of the rectitude of my intentions, I do not covet the praises of the one nor fear the censures of the other. It is at another tribunal that I, as well as other men, are to account for my conduct.'

Thomas Bewick continued to engrave wood almost to the last day of his life, and his sense of humour and the macabre is revealed in the final woodcut vignette he executed just before his death on 8 November 1828 (plate 94).

This vignette shows a view of his birthplace, Cherryburn, with Mickley Bank in the background. A funeral procession descends the steep pasture towards the waiting boat which was to convey them across the Tyne to the family burial ground at Ovingham. A portent of his end – perhaps?

Thus died a patriot and a rebel. Englishmen can be proud of him, but the Americans even more so. Had Thomas Bewick emigrated to America, a move he actually contemplated, he undoubtedly would have been a rebel. In sorrow more than in anger, he would have ridden alongside Paul Revere and who can say what the measure of his greatness would then have been?

153

19 The Happy Glassmakers

In spite of taxation, the Newcastle glassmakers were a happy lot and were to achieve much eminence in the civic affairs of the city. Isaac Cookson was to become Sheriff of Newcastle in 1779.

Another glassmaker, Sir Matthew White Ridley, who had acquired the control of the Henzell glass houses, was twice mayor and became a Member of Parliament on 4 March 1769, and it is recorded that 'on Sunday the bells were set a-ringing on the arrival of the news of Sir Matthew keeping his seat, and on Monday there were great rejoicings in the Low glass houses on that occasion'.

Not content with that, the glassmakers were to hold an election for King of the Glassmakers. This was held at Closegate on 3 October 1789 and the candidates were two very distinguished glassmakers: the Hon. Sir John Turner and the Hon. Sir James Sanders. The result created immense excitement and was very close:

Sir James .. .. .. 500 votes
Sir John .. .. .. 498 votes

Thus, Sir James was elected King of the Glassmakers by a majority of two. An interesting aspect of this election was the number of voters. Only glassworkers were allowed to vote and it gives an indication of the size of the Newcastle glass industry when at this period over one thousand workers at least, were 'continuously employed'.

But everything was not gaiety, as the following extract from the *Newcastle General Advertiser* shows:

Newcastle, 27 December 1753.

'Yesterday in the afternoon, a man going accidently into the Mushroom Glasshouse near this town (Glasshouse Bridge) with a charged fowling-piece in his hand, carelessly laid it down, when Zachary Tyzack, one of the workmen, taking it up, mortally wounded William Randal, another of the said workmen.'

Recording the death of a glassmaker:

Newcastle Chronicle, 18 March, 1769.

'Thursday died at the Low Glass Houses, Mr Joshua Henzell, in the 82nd year of his age. A very worthy and honest man. Though he was esteemed the most corpulent person in this part of the country, yet (till within a few days of his latter end) he always displayed

154

himself in the manual execution of his business, a glass maker. As possessing the abilities of an able workman, united with the alacrity of youth, has thereby acquired a very handsome fortune.'

But the glassmakers were not always honest:

An advertisement in *Newcastle Chronicle*, 4 October 1800, reads: 'Being satisfied of the necessity of prosecuting any servant employed in our different manufactories for stealing or embessling glass and offering it for sale, we do hereby agree to prosecute at our joint expense any such offenders, or any person purchasing such glass knowing it to be stolen, to the utmost rigour of the law.'

Airey, Cookson and Company

Northumberland Glass Company

Richard Turner Shortridge & Company.

The Annual Glassmakers' Procession

The great day in the happy glassmakers' year was their annual procession through the streets of Newcastle. A brilliant record has been preserved of one of these bright and gay occasions, which took place on 12 September 1823. This record is so good, and gives such insight to the times as they were, that it is reproduced in full without deletion or correction:

'September 12 – The inhabitants of Newcastle and Gateshead were gratified with a novel and interesting spectacle, in a procession through the principal streets, of the workman employed in several of the glass-houses in that and the neighbouring towns, each bearing in his hand a specimen of the art, remarkable either for its curious construction or its beauty and elegance. The morning was ushered in with the ringing of bells, and notice of the intended procession having been previously circulated, numbers of people crowded the streets to witness the pleasing spectacle. The yard at the Skinner's burn, belonging to Messrs. Clayton, was the place appointed for the assembling of those who had to form the procession. Here, having been marshalled in due order, a little after twelve o'clock, it moved forward along the Close, amid the cheers of the assembled multitude, the firing of cannon, and the ringing of bells. It was preceded by the band of the Tyne Hussars, and was composed of the workmen of the Northumberland, the South Shields, the Wear (Sunderland), the Durham and British (Gateshead), the Stourbridge (Gateshead), and the North Shields glass companies, arranged according to the seniority of their respective houses, each of which was distinguished by appropriate flags. The sky was clear, and the rays of the sun falling upon the glittering column, gave it a richness and grandeur in appearance that defy description. The hat of almost every person in it was decorated with a glass feather, whilst a glass star sparkled on

155

their breasts, and a chain or collor of variegated glass hung around the neck; some of them also wore sashes round their waist. Each man carried in his hand a staff, on a cross piece on the top of which was displayed one or more curious or beautiful specimens of their art. As these were thus carried above the heads of the crowd, a full view of them was afforded to every one, and the procession was relieved from the inconvenience which might otherwise have been experienced from the populace crowding round it to obtain a sight of the different vessels. These consisted not only of a profusion of decanters, glasses, goblets, jugs, bowls, dishes &c. which may be called the staple articles of the trade, and which exhibited an endless variety of elegant shape and exquisite workmanship, but also of several others, remarkable either for their grandeur and excellence of work, or for the curious nature of their construction: amongst the latter were two elegant bird cages, containing birds, which sang at periods during the procession; a salute was fired several times from a fort mounted with glass cannon, to the astonishment of the spectators; and a glass bugle, which sounded the halts and played several marches, was also much admired for its sweetness and correctness of tone. Several elegant specimens of stained glass were exhibited, and many of the men wore glass hats and carried glass swords. When the procession arrived at the Mansion-house it halted, when a salute was fired from the glass cannon; the procession then moved forward, passing along the bridge to Gateshead, and up the streets of that town as far as Mr Price's house; it then returned and paraded through the principal streets of Newcastle, and finally halted at Mr Thomas Heron's, the Cock Inn, at the head of the Side, where the men belonging to four of the houses were to dine. Here the brittle fort fired a salute, as it had done several times before. The men of the two remaining houses then proceeded to their respective places of entertainment, one to Mrs Wallace's Nag's Head, foot of the Butcher's Bank, the other to Mr. Methuen's, Gateshead. Exhibitions of this kind are highly commendable, not being a mere unmeaning shew calculated for caricature, but exhibiting to public view some of the finest efforts of human industry and genius.'

It has been a great joy to the author that many of the glass ornaments and novelties mentioned and carried in the procession have been traced to the Shipley Art Gallery in Gateshead. These have been photographed by kind permission of the Curator and are reproduced opposite in plate 96.

96 The Glassmakers' Procession
and some of the glass novelties or 'friggers' they carried.
Top hat
Fish
Bell
Pistol
Bellows
Violin
Green walking stick
Drum major's baton
Blue walking stick
Pipe
Shipley Art Gallery
Photograph
Photo-Mayo

157

20 Decline and Glory

It is very hard to pinpoint a moment in time when the great glass industry of Newcastle upon Tyne began to decline. Perhaps it was the increasing stranglehold of taxation which placed a discount on craftsmanship; perhaps it was the development of Britain's transport system, which reduced the value of the old keelboat access to the glass houses and the easy egress to the world markets; perhaps it was the development of Newcastle upon Tyne as a heavy industrial centre with its pioneering links of locomotive and rail; perhaps it was the immense rise of shipbuilding on the Tyne.

But, whatever the cause, the fact had to be faced that, with the nineteenth century drawing to a close, the furnaces of the glass houses were to be doused for ever, one after the other. In the twentieth century, the great glass industry of Newcastle is now virtually ended.

Let us look at the old sites along the Ouseburn, the valley which was once green and lovely, over the Glasshouse Bridge and beyond to Glasshouse Street, where the district was once called 'The Glasshouses' and where the Huguenots worked. From here can be seen the site where the Western glass house once functioned, but it is now an old warehouse, empty and forlorn.

Along the side of the river and from the Western glass house a succession of names come from the past; the Crown glass house, the Middle Bottle glass house, the Middle Broad glass house, the St Lawrence Mushroom glass house and, finally, the St Lawrence glass house. They are all gone leaving no traces.

Standing on the site of the St Lawrence glass house, a vast hulk towers above the level of the terraced houses around the bend in the river – it is the stern of the *Esso Northumbria*, the largest ship ever to be built in Britain and soon to be launched by a Princess of England.

Back to the Glasshouse Bridge, and across the Ouseburn stands Bridge Glassworks, the only survivor in Newcastle of the largest glass centre in the world, but it no longer melts and fashions glass.

From Bridge Glassworks, which stands almost exactly abreast of Hadrian's Wall, we continue our walk to the Old Castle in the centre of a teeming city. The unrelenting walls of the Norman Castle still

158

dominate, and in the gathering dusk we look across to the Cathedral of St Nicholas. Just to the left we see the corner of the churchyard – 'Amen Corner'; from there William and Mary Beilby used to walk through the Black Gate to the Castle, and down the Castle Garth Stairs to meet and work with the glass blowers of Closegate.

Below the shadow of the Old Castle and down the Castle Garth Stairs (plate 49) we reach the Close. Some of the eighteenth-century buildings still survive with their Elizabethan elegance, but we reach a point where a mark in the retaining wall on the north side of the Close indicates that this is where the old City Wall reached the Close, and the actual spot where the old Closegate was situated. What memories of the past this stirs for it is where the old Closegate glass house of Airey, Cookson and Company stood; but there is no trace of it left.

Along the Close, which was once called 'Closegate Without', we walk to Skinnerburn, where the old keelboats used to load the finished glass; and on each side we pass the sites of the old glass houses where the era of elegance in Newcastle Glass was created.

But they are all silent now, and the furnaces no longer glow through the night. The ghosts of the Dagnias, the Cooksons, the Aireys and the Huguenots seem to mingle with the fleeting mists of the river.

And so the glory of Newcastle glass is forever ended.

The ghosts of the river assemble and seem to beckon to a new group – two men and a slight girl. Who could they be but the Beilbys – William and Ralph and Mary. They appear to be quite cheerful, and merge with the others in a happy communion of memories.

Is it so, they seem to say, that our glasses are to be seen in the Victoria and Albert Museum, and the Fitzwilliam and the Ashmolean, and the Cecil Higgins and the Philadelphia and the Corning, and the Laing Art and the Royal Scottish. – Yes indeed they are there! Our glasses, fashioned in Newcastle of finest metal, of elegance and grace and of finely fused colour which we painted. Yes indeed, they are there for all to see – and for all time.

159

160

The Newcastle decanter

97 Sloping shoulder
in flint glass.
Height $9\frac{1}{4}$ in.
Decor: *Reverse* The Arms
of Sir Edward Blackett,
Mayor of Newcastle upon
Tyne, in full colour
enamel, with the inscription
Claret supported by rococo
scroll and fruiting vine in
white enamel.

98
Decor: *Front* The Arms of
the City of Newcastle upon
Tyne, in full colour
enamel with supporting
scroll.
Decorated by William
Beilby, signed and dated
1762.
Victoria and Albert
Museum, London
Photograph
Photo-Mayo

161

Appendixes

A note on the photographs

My very special thanks are due to PHOTO-MAYO LTD of Newcastle upon Tyne who were responsible for nearly all of the beautiful colour photographs in this book. Mr Robert Mayo, on discussing this project with me, agreed that nothing but the finest high-definition colour photography would do justice to the work of the Beilbys; he then carefully briefed his son Bob Mayo to work with me.

Photographing the Beilby specimens has been one of the most rewarding tasks associated with this publication, and with young Bob Mayo I have driven many thousands of miles to beautiful museums and very lovely private homes throughout Britain. Sometimes we would be received kindly and made to feel our task was really worthwhile and sometimes we would be received with reserve and suspicion. Occasionally the reserve would melt and we would leave with a warm feeling of new friends made. Sometimes, the opposition was quite astonishing and on one occasion a veritable 'obstacle course' was placed in our way. But we refused at any time to be deviated from the high standard set.

Not every Beilby glass was actually photographed, but most of them in Britain were, and the joy of seeing the finished brilliant transparencies was reward enough for the sustained effort.

Bob Mayo deserves great praise for his infinite patience and steadfast refusal to be hurried and to carry out any other than a first-class professional job. He very kindly observed, in an off-moment, that I was the best assistant he had ever had.

For the transparencies 10 in. × 8 in. Kodak Ektachrome film was used and our friends in the United States agreed and employed exactly the same, so that a similar all-round colour balance could be achieved. Studio conditions were set up at all locations, eliminating daylight completely and using Colour Tran floodlighting, which enabled us to control not only the intensity (up to 10,000 watts) but also the colour temperature. A Super Cambo studio camera was used with a 360 mm Schneider Symmer lens.

The whole equipment, with tripods, photo floods and electrical

162

accessories, was quite a considerable weight and the moving of it from one museum to another was a veritable *tour de force*, especially when we had an 'obstacle course' to negotiate.

Special Notes

The Arms of Sir Edward Blackett, Mayor of Newcastle upon Tyne, illustrated on the decanter (plates 97 and 98) have a most interesting significance to the author.

On 10 November 1965, the author, as Founder Chairman, signed a lease acquiring Matfen Hall, the ancestral home of the Blackett family, for conversion into a Cheshire Home on behalf of the Cheshire Foundation. The lease was negotiated with and counter-signed by Sir Douglas Blackett, Bart., the descendant of Sir Edward Blackett.

All royalties from this book are donated directly to Matfen Hall, The Northumberland Cheshire Home.

Bibliography

Books

C. E. Adamson
John Dagnia Glassblower,
South Shields, 1894

L. M. Angus Butterworth
British Table and Ornamental Glass,
London, 1956

E. Barrington Haynes
Glass Through the Ages,
London, 1948

Thomas Bewick
Memoir,
London, 1862

L. M. Bickerton
*Eighteenth Century English
Drinking Glasses,*
London, 1972

Joseph Bles
Rare English Glass,
London, 1924

H. Bourne
History of Newcastle,
Newcastle, 1736

John Brand
History of Newcastle,
London, 1789

Francis Buckley
A History of Old English Glass,
London, 1925

Francis Buckley
English Baluster Stemmed Glasses,
Edinburgh (Private), 1912

G. T. Clark
Some Account of Sir Robert Mansel,
Dowlais, 1883

E. Dillon
Glass,
London, 1907

Davis & Middleton
Coloured Glass,
London, 1968

Frank Davis
Glass,
London, 1966

Derek C. Davis
Glass for Collectors,
London, 1971

E. M. Elville
English Table Glass,
London, 1951

E. M. Elville
The Collectors Dictionary of Glass,
London, 1961

A. Hartshorne
Old English Glass,
London, 1897

**W. P. Hedley & C. R.
Hudleston**
The Cookson Family,
Kendal (Private), 1967

W. B. Honey
English Glass,
London, 1946

D. Mackenzie
History of Newcastle,
Newcastle, 1827

C. J. Peddle
Defects in Glass,
London, 1927

W. A. Thorpe
A History of English and Irish Glass,
London, 1929

W. A. Thorpe
Glass,
London, 1935

**Officers of The Victoria and
Albert Museum**
50 Masterpieces of Pottery and Glass,
London, 1950

O. N. Wilkinson
Old Glass,
London, 1968

Geoffrey Wills
Antique Glass,
London, 1971

Richard Welford
Men of Mark, Ralph Beilby,
Newcastle, 1895

Ward Lloyd
Investing in Georgian Glass,
London, 1969

164

Papers and Journals

Francis Buckley
Glasshouses on the Tyne in the Eighteenth Century,
Journal of the Society of Glass Technology, Vol. 10, 1926

Francis Buckley
The Beilby Family,
The Connoisseur, September 1929

R. J. Charleston
Dutch Decoration of English Glass,
Journal of the Society of Glass Technology

R. J. Charleston
A Documentary of Beilby Glass,
The Connoisseur, May 1964

James Clephan
Manufacture of Glass in England. Rise of the Art on the Tyne,
Archaeologia Aeliana, New Series, Newcastle, 1880

Helen Comstock
Beilby Glass in America,
The Connoisseur, May 1951

Preston Pilbin
The Influence of Local Geography on the Glass Industry of Tyneside,
Journal of Tyneside Geographical Society, Newcastle upon Tyne, October 1936

Ursula Ridley
The History of Glass Making on the Tyne & Wear,
Archaeologia Aeliana, Series 4, Newcastle, 1962

W. A. Thorpe
The Dagnia Tradition in Newcastle Glass,
The Connoisseur, 1933

W. A. Thorpe
The Beilby Glasses,
The Connoisseur, Vol. 81, 1928

Various
Three references in The Gentleman's Magazine, 1814

William Beilby's death notice, Hull Advertiser, 9 October 1819

Entry in the Hull Directory, 1817

Thomas Beilby entry in the Leeds Mercury, 22 June 1773

Mrs Ralph Beilby's letter, Literary and Philosophical Society of Newcastle upon Tyne, 28 December 1822

Onesiphorus Dagnia entry in the London Gazette, 9 May 1786

Various references in the Newcastle Chronicle, Eighteenth Century issues

Various references in the Newcastle Courant, Eighteenth Century issues

Entry in the Treasury Papers, 1697 XC 112

Ralph Beilby, last will and testament, Department of Palaeography University of Durham, 25 November 1816

Dagnia references, Proceedings of the Newcastle Society of Antiquaries (4 Scr VI)

Entry in the Directory of Newcastle upon Tyne, 1778

Entry in the Directory of Newcastle upon Tyne, 1779

Entry in the Directory of Newcastle upon Tyne, 1790

Entry in the Directory of Newcastle upon Tyne, 1801

Entry in the Directory of Newcastle upon Tyne, 1811

Maps

Corbridge
Newcastle upon Tyne,
1723, Newcastle Central Library

Henry Bourne
Newcastle upon Tyne,
1736, Newcastle Central Library

Izaac Thompson
Newcastle upon Tyne,
1746, Newcastle Central Library

Charles Hutton
Newcastle upon Tyne,
1770, Newcastle Central Library

Ralph Beilby
Newcastle upon Tyne,
1788, Newcastle Central Library

John Wood
Newcastle upon Tyne,
1827, Newcastle Central Library

T. Oliver
Newcastle upon Tyne
1830, Newcastle Central Library

Plan
Airey Cookson Glasshouse,
1802, Newcastle Central Library

Glossary

Air Twist Stem
In which glass threads are drawn from the clear glass metal and twisted to form many varied and intricate patterns in the stem

Amen Corner
The South East Corner of the Cathedral Church of Saint Nicholas, Newcastle, and where Ralph and William Beilby established their workshop

Baluster Stem
In which baluster effects are introduced into the stem, sometimes upright and sometimes inverted

Blewyglasse Clay
The fine clay used by the glassmakers for their pots and which was found in Northumberland

Closegate
The Western entrance to the Walled City of Newcastle alongside the river and entering the fashionable medieval street called The Close
Demolished in *1797*

Closegate Without
An area outside the Closegate and the City Wall but still within the administrative boundary of the Common Council of Newcastle

Common Council of Newcastle
The administrative authority of Newcastle upon Tyne before the Municipal Reform Act of 1835

Enamel Firing
When the glass metal almost reaches melting point and where the enamel pigments virtually become part of the glass

Firing Glass
The short, squat and heavy stemmed or semi-stemmed glasses used for toasting and for 'firing' which was the rhythmic knocking on the table to approve the toast

Flint Glass
Another description of Lead Crystal

Folded Foot
In which the foot fringe of glass metal is folded underneath to present a more solid and firm platform for the glass

Glafs
The old English spelling of Glass

Glass Blooming
The clouding of glass metal during processing, and which usually is caused by fumes from the furnace reaching the melt

'Invt'
Latin abbreviation for *designed*

Keel Boats
The shallow bottomed boats used on the Tyne to convey coal to the markets of the country and the world

Lead Crystal
Glass usually made with a lead oxide content of 31 per cent

Lead Oxide
The great discovery of George Ravencroft, in 1691. By introducing a carefully balanced proportion of lead oxide into the glass melt it created brilliant white crystal glass and was to make English Lead Crystal the finest glass in the world

Metal
Glass mix in either its solid or liquid viscous state

Newcastle upon Tyne
Originally a Roman military crossing of the Tyne called Pons Eeli.
Named Newcastle from 1080.
Became a Cathedral City in 1882.
For all purposes in this book referred to as a City

Opaque Twist Stem
Similar process as in air twist excepting that the threads are of opaque glass to give a brilliant contrasting effect within the stem

Ouseburn
A tributary of the Tyne to the East of Newcastle

'Pinxt'
Latin abbreviation for *painted*

Ratafia Glass
A glass for cordial, of very small fluid ounce capacity, but usually with an extremely tall tapering bowl and drawn stem

Skinnerburn
A very small tributary of the Tyne to the West of Newcastle

White Glasshouse
Another expression for the term Flint Glasshouse

166

Index